# BOOST YOUR
# GROWTHDNA

## HOW STRATEGIC LEADERS
## USE GROWTH GENETICS
## TO DRIVE SUSTAINABLE
## BUSINESS PERFORMANCE

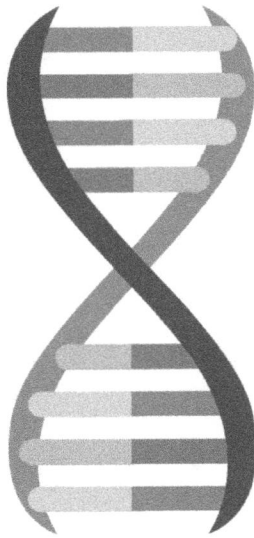

## Margaret Reynolds

INDIE BOOKS
INTERNATIONAL

# DEDICATION

*To my friends at the Helzberg Entrepreneurial Mentoring Program, who are committed to boosting the GrowthDNA of every mentee.*

ISBN-10: 1-947480-68-5
ISBN-13: 978-1-947480-68-1
Library of Congress Control Number: 2019911338


GROWTHDNA is a registered trademark of Reynolds Consulting, LLC

Designed by Joni McPherson, mcphersongraphics.com

INDIE BOOKS INTERNATIONAL, INC
2424 VISTA WAY, SUITE 316
OCEANSIDE, CA 92054
www.indiebooksintl.com

# TABLE OF CONTENTS

Foreword. . . . . . . . . . . . . . . . . . . . . . . . . . . . . . . . . . . . . . . vii

**PART I: Why Growth Matters**. . . . . . . . . . . . . . . . . . . . . . 1

  **Chapter 1:** Business Growth Is Elusive. . . . . . . . . . . . . . . 3
    Chapter Summary . . . . . . . . . . . . . . . . . . . . . 7
    Key Questions. . . . . . . . . . . . . . . . . . . . . . . . 8

  **Chapter 2:** The Traditional Approach To Growth Is
  All Wrong . . . . . . . . . . . . . . . . . . . . . . . . . . . . . 9
    Chapter Summary . . . . . . . . . . . . . . . . . . . . . 13
    Key Questions. . . . . . . . . . . . . . . . . . . . . . . . 13

**PART 2: What Is GrowthDNA?**. . . . . . . . . . . . . . . . . . . 15

  **Chapter 3:** Businesses Have DNA . . . . . . . . . . . . . . . . . 17
    Chapter Summary . . . . . . . . . . . . . . . . . . . . . 24
    Key Questions. . . . . . . . . . . . . . . . . . . . . . . . 25

  **Chapter 4:** ConfidenceDNA Is Based On Market
  Intelligence . . . . . . . . . . . . . . . . . . . . . . . . . . . . 27
    Chapter Summary . . . . . . . . . . . . . . . . . . . . . 36
    Key Questions. . . . . . . . . . . . . . . . . . . . . . . . 37

  **Chapter 5:** ClarityDNA Is Created Through Strategy. . . 39
    Chapter Summary . . . . . . . . . . . . . . . . . . . . . 45
    Key Questions. . . . . . . . . . . . . . . . . . . . . . . . 46

  **Chapter 6:** CommitmentDNA Emanates From
  Leadership. . . . . . . . . . . . . . . . . . . . . . . . . . . . . 47
    Chapter Summary . . . . . . . . . . . . . . . . . . . . . 54
    Key Questions. . . . . . . . . . . . . . . . . . . . . . . . 55

  **Chapter 7:** CultureDNA Drives Performance . . . . . . . . 57
    Chapter Summary . . . . . . . . . . . . . . . . . . . . . 64
    Key Questions. . . . . . . . . . . . . . . . . . . . . . . . 66

**PART 3: How GrowthDNA Works** . . . . . . . . . . . . . . . . . . . . 67

  **Chapter 8:** Maximizing GrowthDNA Results . . . . . . . . 69
    Chapter Summary . . . . . . . . . . . . . . . . . . . . . . . 72
    Key Questions . . . . . . . . . . . . . . . . . . . . . . . . . . 72

  **Chapter 9:** GrowthDNA Is Cyclical. . . . . . . . . . . . . . . 73
    Chapter Summary . . . . . . . . . . . . . . . . . . . . . . . 85
    Key Questions . . . . . . . . . . . . . . . . . . . . . . . . . . 87

  **Chapter 10:** GrowthDNA Is Cumulative . . . . . . . . . . . 89
    Chapter Summary: . . . . . . . . . . . . . . . . . . . . . . . 91
    Key Questions: . . . . . . . . . . . . . . . . . . . . . . . . . 91

  **Chapter 11:** GrowthDNA Diagnoses Growth Limiters . . 93
    Chapter Summary . . . . . . . . . . . . . . . . . . . . . . . 96
    Key Questions . . . . . . . . . . . . . . . . . . . . . . . . . . 97

**PART 4: The GrowthDNA Experience.** . . . . . . . . . . . . . . . 99

  **Chapter 12:** GrowthDNA Case Studies . . . . . . . . . . . . 101
    Chapter Summary . . . . . . . . . . . . . . . . . . . . . . . 121
    Key Questions . . . . . . . . . . . . . . . . . . . . . . . . . . 121

**Appendix A: The GrowthDNA Scorecard Assessment.** . . 123
  Overall GrowthDNA Scoring . . . . . . . . . . . . . . . . . . . 125
  GrowthDNA Strand Scores. . . . . . . . . . . . . . . . . . . . . 125
  GrowthDNA Scores Correlate With Performance. . . . . 127
  GrowthDNA Alignment Within A Company . . . . . . . . 127

**Appendix B: Chapter Summaries** . . . . . . . . . . . . . . . . . . . 129

**Appendix C: Chapter Key Questions** . . . . . . . . . . . . . . . . 139

**Appendix D: Works Referenced** . . . . . . . . . . . . . . . . . . . . 145

**Appendix E: Acknowledgments** . . . . . . . . . . . . . . . . . . . . 149

**Appendix F: About the Author** . . . . . . . . . . . . . . . . . . . . 153

**Appendix G: Index.** . . . . . . . . . . . . . . . . . . . . . . . . . . . . . . 155

# FOREWORD

This book may change the growth of your organization, depending on your personal commitment.

Our family business, Helzberg Diamonds, was founded in 1915. The company grew from fifteen units in 1962 to the third largest jewelry retailer in the United States with more than 100 stores in twenty-three states by 1995. The most successful people want to be the best in their industry, rather than the richest, and they balance family time with company time. I was not a perfect example of this and want to share this caveat with you. I learned from Vivian Jennings of Rainy Day Books in Fairway, Kansas, that "Bigger isn't better; better is better."

The loyal executive team was nearing retirement, and it was important to ensure that the family business and its dedicated long-term associates would continue to prosper. After my chance meeting on the streets of New York with Warren Buffett, the company was acquired by Berkshire Hathaway, one of the most honored companies on the planet. This ensured the financial base of the company and the ability to continue to progress.

The company learned a lot about growth. Mistakes contributed to our learning and success. This was not accomplished without some degree of pain along the way.

Having been lucky enough to work with our excellent team that created the Helzberg Diamonds' success, the Helzberg Entrepreneurial Mentoring Program (HEMP) was founded in 1995. HEMP was also based on my personal experience with Ewing Marion Kauffman, the founder of Marion Laboratories and the owner of the Kansas City Royals. Mr. K, as he was known, became my mentor for twenty-three years. One day when I thanked him, he said, "You'll help somebody someday." That provided the inspiration for starting HEMP.

HEMP matches seasoned, successful entrepreneurial mentors like Margaret Reynolds, the author of this book (formerly a top executive at Hallmark Cards, Inc.), with less-experienced entrepreneurs. Wonderful mentoring and sharing are fostered through peer-to-peer relationships derived from involvement in their membership.

HEMP has graduated more than 300 business leaders, and their businesses have grown on average over 40 percent. HEMP applies some very simple time-tested principles: mainly, *put your worst foot forward* paired with *absolute confidentiality.*

Margaret Reynolds has been one of our go-to mentors in the area of growth for over a decade, helping mentees put their problems and concerns forward. Margaret has handled difficult situations with honesty and a strong voice.

Her principles work. Based on workshop reviews from our HEMP members, it is quite clear our HEMPers have tremendously benefited from Margaret's expertise.

Margaret has the ability to take complex business problems to the root of the issue and provide systematic solutions. Guided by Margaret's wisdom, I am confident this book, along with your commitment and efforts, will help your organization progress.

Happy reading. I wish you great success and enjoyment with the growth of your organization and the increasing benefits to your associates and your family.

*Barnett Helzberg, Jr.*
*Former owner, president, and chairman of Helzberg Diamonds,*
*Chairman of the Board, The Helzberg Entrepreneurial Mentoring*
*Program HEMP*

# PART I

# Why
# Growth
# Matters

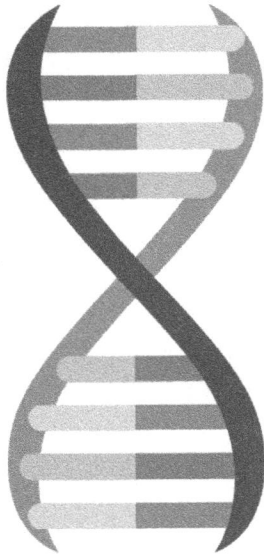

# CHAPTER 1

# Business Growth
# Is Elusive

Company leaders worldwide seek business growth for many reasons. Whether it is to expand profitability to drive shareholder value, to build stronger market value in preparation for a transaction, or to allow them to support and promote their employees (and by extension their families and community), growth is desirable for just about every organization. So, why is it so elusive?

Would it surprise you to know that only 13 percent of companies are able to sustain a relatively modest single-digit growth rate for ten or more years?[1] What about the rest? They invest inordinate amounts of time and money while enduring substantial stress trying to create a growth trajectory that they believe is consistent with the potential of the organization, often with mixed or disappointing results.

For many of us, as leaders, the business is run through the management of two things: financial reports and operations. We are taught in business school that these things are important, and managing them has been rewarded in our careers as we mastered them. Yet, neither are growth-generating activities. They typically focus the organization on operational improvements or cost savings. At best, they may generate

---

[1] Chris Zook, *Beyond the Core: Expand Your Market without Abandoning Your Roots* (Boston, MA: Harvard Business School Press, 2004).

single-digit incremental improvement, extending the current baseline, but not changing its trajectory.

An article titled "Stop Focusing on Profitability and Go for Growth," published in *Harvard Business Review* in 2017, revealed the rise in intrinsic equity value from a 1 percent increase in growth is about five times larger than the same increase in pretax operating profit.[2] As growth-oriented leaders, we have to ask ourselves, how much of our time are we spending on managing for tomorrow versus managing for today? The article's author, Michael Mankins, says, "We hear CEOs describe one or two bets—at most—on growth while devoting most of their time to showcasing the results of restructuring, offshoring, and other cost-focused initiatives."

# Growth Or Profit?

## RETURN IN EQUITY VALUE ON 1 PERCENT INCREASE

| Industry | Long-Term Growth | Pretax Operating Profit |
|---|---|---|
| Services | 19% | 4% |
| Equipment and Manufacturing | 18% | 4% |
| Chemicals, Metals and Raw Materials | 18% | 5% |

FIGURE 1.1

My work with clients illustrates the same point. For example, when speaking at a conference of business owners recently, I asked one of the board members, well respected for running a tight ship, if I could review the key measures that he and his team rely on to run the business. Out of eighty-four measures tracked, 74 percent were focused on cutting expenses, while 26 percent were about driving the top line (see Figure 1.2, Metrics

---

[2] Michael Mankins, "Stop Focusing on Profitability and Go for Growth," *Harvard Business Review*, September 20, 2017, https://hbr.org/2017/05/stop-focusing-on-profitability-and-go-for-growth.

Tracked). That may not sound like a bad ratio, but half of the top-line measures were not about changing the top line, but simply tracking it.

Most revenue measures, taken from financial spreadsheets, are outcome measures. They are the results of other actions. That makes them *lagging indicators*. They are finite and static. Once recorded, they are in the past. The ideal growth measures are *leading indicators*, which are the behaviors and activities that predict or drive revenue growth. Don't misunderstand. I advocate for both operational and growth metrics. But as leaders who are in a unique position to change the future of the company, if we are not working on growth, who is? It isn't hard to connect the dots—if we are not championing many growth initiatives and we are not tracking growth goals, we are probably not going to achieve them.

### METRICS TRACKED

| | Metrics | | Indicators | |
|---|---|---|---|---|
| | Revenue | Expense | Lead | Lag |
| Revenue | 11 | | | 11 |
| Growth | 2 | 2 | | |
| Net Growth | 3 | | 1 | 2 |
| Cost of Goods | | 10 | 4 | 6 |
| Plant | | 24 | 5 | 21 |
| Service | 4 | 10 | 4 | 10 |
| Stockroom | 1 | 18 | 2 | 17 |
| Sales Dept. | 1 | | 1 | |
| Total: 84 Percentage | 22 26% | 62 74% | 17 20% | 67 80% |

FIGURE 1.2

What causes us to stay focused on the operating side of the business? From the time we were young, we have spent our lives conquering the *whats*—the practices and policies that others before us painstakingly put in place, and we were taught to respect. We do what we do because we are supposed to do it. Our parents raised us to, or our teachers taught us to, or our leaders rewarded us when we did. The problem is that the *whats* perpetuate behaviors that began years ago, for just reasons, and have not been re-examined to reflect changing times. Focusing on expenses and operational improvements does not question the fundamental strategic principles of a business, which may have made sense a few decades ago but are today being challenged by changing value systems, new technology, and the shifting of power into the hands of data users.

*Understanding the why behind the action is a more strategic and growth-oriented way to lead and manage the business.*

If business growth is a goal, it is not achieved by a focus on operating profit margins. Both are important. But ask yourself, which of these can only be accomplished by leadership? Leaders must focus on growth and charge managers with controlling margins. If leaders want to change the growth pattern, they must challenge how they manage and where they spend their time. It is critical to spend as much or more time studying and understanding market trends and behaviors as it is to manage internal functions. To nurture growth, question current operating approaches, always asking if the status quo—how we do things—makes sense in light of changing market conditions. Understanding the *why* behind the action is a more strategic and growth-oriented way to lead and manage the business. It enables discerning leaders to separate the wheat from the chaff internally, keeping practices that are still relevant, and changing those that are not.

## CHAPTER SUMMARY

1. While growth is an important goal for most companies, only a small minority of them (approximately 13 percent) are effective at sustaining growth over time.

2. The rise in intrinsic equity value from a 1-percent increase in growth is about five times larger than the same increase in pretax operating profit.

3. Even growth-minded leaders spend the majority of their time focused on operational improvements and financial management and much *less* time on growth initiatives.

4. As leaders, it is critical we spend as much or more time studying and understanding the market trends and behaviors than examining our internal functions.

## KEY QUESTIONS

1. What is your company's growth track record? Is it meeting or exceeding the average for your industry?

2. How much of your time (and that of other key people) is focused on managing day-to-day operations versus driving growth initiatives? Are you satisfied with that distribution of your most valuable asset—time?

3. To what extent does your organization routinely examine the "why" behind the "what"? In other words, do you approach growth by building on what you have, assuming that extending the past is the answer—or do you look at what the market is telling you and define what is possible for your organization before setting goals and objectives?

## CHAPTER 2

# The Traditional Approach To Growth Is All Wrong

One of the many *whats* we learned along the way is that growth initiatives are a key outcome of strategic planning; no debate with that. The problem is that most strategic plans don't generate results. In fact, 70–90 percent of plans fail to achieve their intended outcomes, depending on which study you read. Is it because strategic planning is wrong? Of course not. It is just misunderstood.

Let's face it, most leaders don't get to the corner office because they are experts in strategic planning. Their expertise is most likely to come from the operational or financial side of the business. Their ability to deliver results and beat last year's performance with the current business model gets them there. Yet once there, the role and expectations are different. Now, instead of operating inside a functional area with which they are deeply familiar, they are expected to be able to find new ways to grow the entire organization year after year.

Given the leader's familiarity with the current business, the strategic plan is usually built on the foundation of how to improve what already exists—a focus on the *whats*—rather than determining the potential of the business—the *what-ifs*. What are the signs of an ineffective strategic growth plan?

**Generated in a one- or two-day offsite meeting.** The future of the business is too important to be debated and decided in a brief meeting. This type of planning may involve a SWOT Analysis (strengths, weaknesses, opportunities, and threats) but rarely uses much supporting data to guide assumptions made. As a result, this type of approach is experience-based, meaning it perpetuates the past with all of its historical bias, and promotes currently popular ideas rather than identifying market-defined growth opportunities. It generally produces a list of activities for the company to work on; rarely is it strategic or likely to change the growth pattern.

**Motivated by budget planning.** Strategy motivated by budget is an oxymoron. A strategy is not a number. Strategy defines where a company is going and how it will get there. While linking resources to strategic priorities is critical, the annual budgeting process will not identify market potential or lead to new creative solutions to the market's ever-changing needs. In a survey my company conducted with manufacturers, 78 percent reported doing a strategic plan in the last twelve months, which suggests those are not strategic plans at all, but rather lists of actions tied to budgets.

**Creates lists of departmental projects focused on departmental improvements.** Many strategic plans I see are a composite of department-level goals. The challenge is there is no cohesive strategy holding them together. The fundamental and overarching strategy for the company is missing. When that happens, the organization is set up for competing priorities that stretch resources and yield internal conflict.

**Considered a process rather than an outcome.** A strategic plan process doesn't produce results; strategic implementation does. A strategic plan shouldn't be an event; it should be a dynamic road map for the company that guides actions toward outcomes. The value begins after the plan is written. Successful leaders are strategic leaders who are focused on strategy every day.

**Doesn't describe how the organization will accomplish its plan.** Strategy is the concept that dictates *how* the organization will achieve its goals. It is a choice, which means that it is intended to provide clear focus, not only on what to do but what not to do.

**Is static until time to do the next one.** The majority of strategic plans are shelved almost immediately upon completion because leadership has not linked the goals with daily actions and behaviors. Without understanding what to do differently, the organization simply reverts to doing the same old things.

**Market intelligence focuses on internal data.** Strategy should always be externally focused because it can only succeed if the market buys in. Sales and profitability analysis, the most common type of input into strategic planning, is usually a backward-looking analysis of how a company has performed. It must be balanced with input from customers, through surveys and customer segment dissection, to learn what is working and, importantly, what isn't. Data on industry patterns and general market trends will help interpret the customer data analysis and guide identification of new opportunities. Yet, as can be seen below, the vast majority of inputs into strategic planning tend to be internal and point-in-time, instead of external and forward-looking.

STRATEGIC PLANNING INPUTS

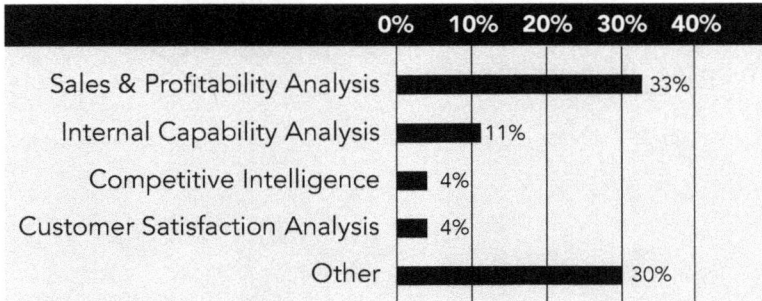

FIGURE 2.1

Strategic plans are a tool. And like any tool, they are wide-ranging in their effectiveness. Some plans work, but most don't. What, then, is the right approach to driving growth?

The key to understanding the gap between desiring growth and achieving it is not found in the actions of the organizations which pursue it. A strategic plan by itself won't help you grow; it is a plan on paper. Some say, "Culture eats strategy for breakfast," and yet even a great culture won't turn the company around if the product isn't innovative enough to capture market attention. All the hard work in the world won't make a customer buy. At the end of the day, the results being achieved are the realistic outcome of the activities we perform *and* the way they are performed.

If leaders want to be champions for growth in their organizations, they must understand it isn't the *whats* or the activities themselves that matter; it is how organizations approach them. A company can do everything "right" and still have very limited success. The sole source of growth, regardless of industry, is the organic conformation of the company, its genetic coding—its DNA.

> *If leaders want to be champions for growth in their organizations, they must understand it isn't the* whats *or the activities themselves that matter; it is how organizations approach them.*

## CHAPTER SUMMARY

1. Strategic planning often doesn't yield growth.

2. Strategic planning, like other management tools, is often viewed as a process, not an outcome.

3. Growth is the result of the way an organization undertakes activities, not the activities themselves.

4. Every organization has DNA that influences *how* they get things done; it is the DNA that separates those which are successful from those which are not.

## KEY QUESTIONS

1. How effective has your organization's strategic planning been when measured by results?

2. Is your strategic planning work a static, occasional process, or does strategy drive day-to-day work?

3. Can you define your organization's DNA?

# PART 2

# What Is GrowthDNA?

CHAPTER 3

# Businesses Have DNA

Human DNA testing exploded in 2017, more than doubling. Today, around one in twenty-five adult Americans have access to their personal genetic data.[3] A survey by Counsyl, a health technology company based in San Francisco, indicates that 53 percent of American consumers want to know what is in their DNA.[4] What drives the need to know?

According to the founder and CEO of Counsyl, Ramji Srinivasan, this is because early awareness of risk can make a big difference in health outcomes. There is an interest in being proactive about something so essential.[5] Srinivasan says DNA is essentially a predictor of what is possible. It increases the odds of a potential outcome.

><
*DNA is essentially a predictor of what is possible. It increases the odds of a potential outcome.*
><

What exactly is DNA? The DNA molecule is a double helix: that is, two long, thin strands twisted around each other like

---

[3] Antonio Regalado, "2017 Was the Year Consumer DNA Testing Blew Up." MIT Technology Review, February 13, 2018. https://www.technologyreview.com/s/610233/2017-was-the-year-consumer-dna-testing-blew-up/.

[4] "Genetic Screening and Support for Women and Their Families," Myriad Women's Health, https://myriadwomenshealth.com/.

[5] "New Survey Finds Majority of Americans Want to Know What's in Their DNA," Business Wire, September 24, 2015, https://www.businesswire.com/news/home/20150924005346/en/New-Survey-Finds-Majority-Americans-What's-DNA.

a spiral staircase. An organism's DNA affects how it looks, how it behaves, and its physiology. The primary role of DNA in the cell is the long-term storage of information. Researchers have found that epigenetic marks on DNA—chemical marks other than the DNA sequence—do indeed change over a person's lifetime, and that the degree of change is similar among family members. So, a change in an organism's DNA can cause changes in all aspects of its life.

Like humans, organizations also have distinct DNA—a genetic imprint that determines outcomes. Fortunately for growth goals, your business DNA can be altered over its lifetime to drive improved growth results. That DNA consists of how people approach problems, how work is defined, how decisions are made, and how communication takes place.

One of the challenges for leaders is understanding their DNA, as it is invisible and lies below the surface of the organization. It expresses itself in how things are done, but it is not limited to culture. It's a composite of how the organization thinks and works, expressed through behaviors and processes. For example, companies that are highly rote and scripted, mired in tradition, struggle more with growth than those that are more strategic in their thinking and participatory in their behaviors.

> *DNA is invisible and lies below the surface of the organization.*

**GrowthDNA** is a framework designed to help leaders identify the unseen variables in their organizations: the DNA that contributes to or detracts from the growth of the company. (Just as after your personal DNA is tested, you can begin to manage and even modify your current DNA structure, strengthening latent DNA and leveraging DNA strands that are assets.) Proactively managing your business DNA greatly increases the odds for a healthier business outcome and performance sustainability.

As with human DNA, to manage outcomes, you must first understand your company's unique genetic code. We have created a GrowthDNA scorecard assessment that enables leaders to identify the current DNA conformation. The test provides a score for each of the four strands of GrowthDNA as well as an overall score.

*Fortunately for growth goals, your business DNA can be altered over its lifetime to drive improved growth results.*

In GrowthDNA testing to date, our results show most companies which take the assessment score in an average range; they have some areas of DNA strength and other areas in need of improvement. High-performance companies, however, score higher. They average 26 percent higher overall. Finally, clients who have worked to improve their DNA score 15 percent higher still. (For a more detailed understanding of this tool, including peer comparisons, see appendix A. The reader will benefit even more by taking the assessment at www.dnascorecard.com before continuing to chapter 4.)

## GrowthDNA Strands

There are four essential DNA strands, or components, of GrowthDNA. Each of these strands is distinct, but also interconnected. *All four GrowthDNA strands must be boosted to achieve sustainable and significant growth results.*

**ConfidenceDNA.** Without confidence, bold moves are unlikely to happen. Companies without confidence don't push themselves out of their comfort zone. They don't challenge existing boundaries and don't believe they can overcome barriers. In order to generate confidence, an organization must have outside-in, focused market intelligence. Such organizations regularly track macro trends, such as technological advances, value shifts in their customer base, and customer problems that need to be solved. They are aware of what competitors are doing, not so they can emulate them, but so they know how to differentiate from them. It is this data that unveils opportunities for growth that are often ignored or overlooked by organizations that manage the business based on operational and financial results. Furthermore, using data to drive decisions helps create cross-functional alignment, as facts put leaders across the organization on the same page and minimize the emotional and experiential forces that can create bias and conflict. *ConfidenceDNA comes from using market data to challenge the status quo and deciding what capabilities to build on, where business weaknesses relative to market needs are, and what new opportunities exist.*

**ClarityDNA.** Clarity is one of those things that sounds easy but is really hard. You have a clear vision, so why isn't the company implementing it? Often, the vision may be clear, but the journey (how to get there) is not. An effective strategy requires clarity on not just where the organization is going, but also how it will get there. Every stakeholder, from boards to front-line employees, must understand what the strategy is, how it will be implemented, and how their role supports success. Clarity doesn't happen in a day. It takes careful study of collected data to evaluate the opportunities and to determine the best fit for the future course of the organization. Once the company's future potential is defined, in order to achieve clarity, leaders must make a choice about *how* to achieve it—or how they will win in the market they choose to serve. Essentially, an organization has to decide not only what it will do, but what it won't do. That strategic focus is essential not only to achieving results but accelerating them. *ClarityDNA comes from crafting a specific, well-defined strategy that is clear to all responsible for its success.*

**CommitmentDNA**. Plans don't create value, activities do. The entire organization, every person, needs to be committed to doing their part to implement the vision. They become invested when they understand how their role and actions will make a differ-ence. Unfortunately, in most organizations, the development of a strategy doesn't change the work of the organization. People con-tinue to do what they always have done. Generating company-wide commitment takes leadership effort to translate the strategy into actionable priorities that drive resource allocation. Every-one in the organization needs to understand these priorities and how their department and/or role supports them. The key tool leaders have to accomplish this goal is communication. I have yet to meet an employee, however, who thinks communication in his or her organization is sufficient. Most want more frequent and more detailed communication. Inherent in that communication is the need to inspire and moti-vate the employee base and oth-

> *Unfortunately, in most organizations, the development of a strategy doesn't change the work of the organization.*

ers critical to the effective implementation of the priorities. That is an ongoing, everyday responsibility of leadership. *Commit-mentDNA begins at the top and is the number one goal of leadership.*

**CultureDNA.** Now that the organization understands where it is going and what it will take to get there, the goal is to build growth-mindedness into the day-to-day operations of the company. Growth becomes part of the lifeblood of the company and it is everyone's job to think about it, contribute to it, and support it. New processes, new behaviors, and new practices are required to create and sustain a growth-minded organization. Growth-minded organizations are more engaging and participatory, leveraging the collective brain trust of all contributors. Employees are not just empowered, but challenged and held accountable for results over activities. Without this essential piece, organizations get a temporary boost from a strategic plan, but may fall back into hereditary habits. Your organization may have a well-defined, value-driven culture, or one of default, born of the collective personalities of its leaders. Regardless, as the GrowthDNA scorecard reveals, what many leaders believe is a good culture—value-driven with happy employees—doesn't necessarily translate to business success. Growth-mindedness doesn't replace a value-driven culture, but rather embeds the genetic sequencing for it into the existing culture in the form of growth behaviors and practices. *It is CultureDNA that enables organizations to sustain growth year after year.*

### GrowthDNA Framework

The following chart depicts the GrowthDNA framework. The four strands form the circle, which represents an ongoing cycle of improvement. The business capability that boosts the performance of each strand is in the outer circle, along with the benefits to be derived from successful modification of *how* that capability is applied. For example, effective market intelligence yields market insights for growth, defines specific growth opportunities, and the data analyzed creates leadership alignment around a common view of the market and the future potential of the organization.

The four GrowthDNA strands are in the inner circle and define the genetic code needed to maximize growth and achieve sustainable business performance. The higher the level of DNA for each strand, the higher the business performance.

Part 3 of this book provides a more detailed explanation of how GrowthDNA works.

## GROWTHDNA FRAMEWORK

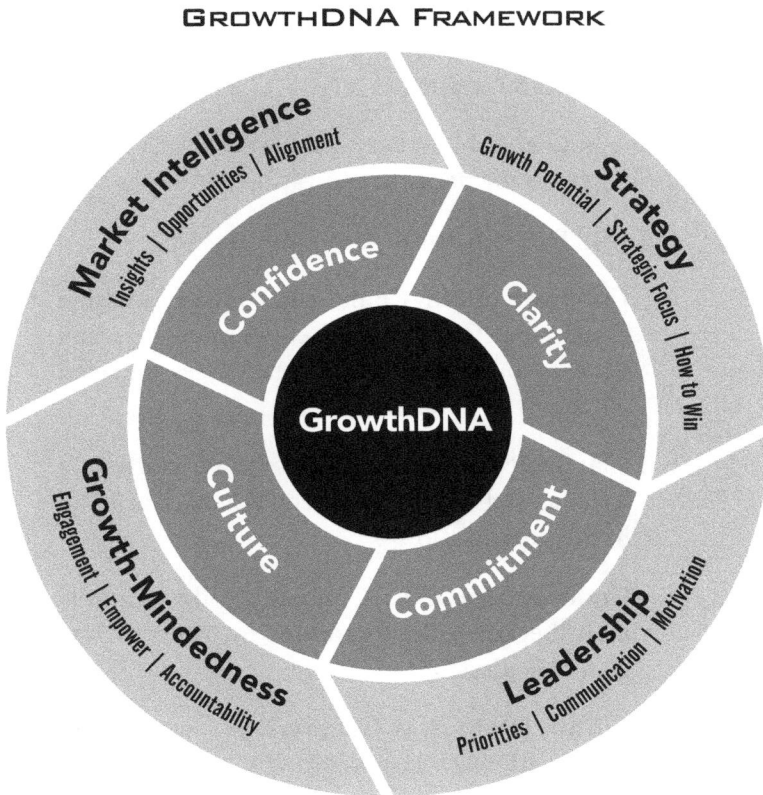

FIGURE 3.1

## CHAPTER SUMMARY

1. Knowing your DNA, personal or organizational, helps you understand how you are wired, which in turn enables you to proactively manage and even change outcomes.

2. GrowthDNA is a framework designed to help leaders identify the variables in their organizations—the DNA—that contribute to or detract from the growth of the company.

3. GrowthDNA testing reveals that awareness of organizational DNA can lead to substantially improved DNA results.

4. There is an alignment between GrowthDNA scores and high-performance organizational growth.

5. GrowthDNA consists of four DNA strands:

   a. **ConfidenceDNA:** Confidence comes from using market data to challenge the status quo, deciding what to build on, where weaknesses are, and what new opportunities exist.

   b. **ClarityDNA:** Clarity comes from crafting a specific, well-defined strategy that is clear to all in the organization.

   c. **CommitmentDNA:** Company-wide commitment begins at the top and is the number one goal of leadership.

   d. **CultureDNA:** It is CultureDNA that enables organizations to sustain growth year after year.

## KEY QUESTIONS

1. Which of the GrowthDNA strands do you think would be your organization's strength?

2. Which of the GrowthDNA strands do you think would be your organization's weakest link?

3. How growth-minded do you think your culture is?

## CHAPTER 4

# ConfidenceDNA Is Based On Market Intelligence

The source of information on which important decisions are made is critical to success. In today's business environment, where most organizations are pressed for time and leaders have years of industry experience, business decisions are often made using executive insight and industry standards. The problem with that is that past experience is not always relevant, given the accelerating pace of market change. Relentless market pressure often requires the organization to take a different approach—an outside-in approach—to developing growth strategy and solving daily business problems. Business leaders need relevant market facts, not anecdotes, and a solid understanding of what customers want, rather than what is easy to provide. Significant growth doesn't come from doing something slightly better than competitors. Often it requires looking at what is going on beyond the industry in which the organization competes to adapt and apply new ideas. Market intelligence is more than internal operational knowledge about the company; it includes comprehensive data about the external market served, with insights about what is expected and desired by today's customers.

The days of answering the phone and picking up sales from loyal customers who want to buy what they bought last year (and the year before) are moving into the rear-view mirror. We need to get in front of where our customers want to go and help them get there with new and creative solutions to their problems that use existing products in new ways, or new products with more integrated service features. Regardless of industry, our customers are significantly pressured to manage margins, and advantages in product differentiation are getting harder to come by. Customers want and expect more value. Most of us assume that means we need to sharpen the pencil and cut price. But is that really the way to add value?

*Market intelligence is more than internal operational knowledge about the company; it includes comprehensive data about the external market served, with insights about what is expected and desired by today's customers.*

A client conducted some powerful research; the results uncovered that excellent customer service isn't enough to grow business with an existing account. It may help you retain what you have, but if you are pursuing growth, you have to identify and solve your customers' problems. What customer problem should you solve? That is where data comes in. What are the goals your customers are being held accountable for? What makes or costs your customers money? If you are in chemical refining, your customers are looking for uptime. In auto repair, customers need throughput. In retail, customers must turn more inventory in the same space. If your product is designed to solve their problem, you will realize added value and very likely extend your relationship while increasing sales volume.

A fast-growing trend that is adding new revenue streams to traditional manufacturers is the addition of services. Apple, one of the most successful trend leaders in product development, is planning to grow by offering services— entertainment apps, credit cards, news, and gaming. This is a notable shift for this product-leadership company.[6] Of course, these services will integrate with and help further differentiate Apple's products. The move is driven by the desire to maintain growth momentum recently slowed by the softening of iPhone sales. It also gives this tech giant the opportunity to leverage loyal followers into new solutions that increase their reliance on all things Apple.

> *If you are pursuing growth, you have to identify and solve your customers' problems.*

Services are not necessarily just add-ons. They are a means of developing relationships with customers at a higher level in the organization, and of adding more value. Services, particularly those that provide solutions to customers' problems, have the potential to become the primary driver of the sale. Solutions from manufacturers usually have three components—a product, a value-adding service (like training), and some kind of ongoing systemic management, like artificial intelligence or data collection.

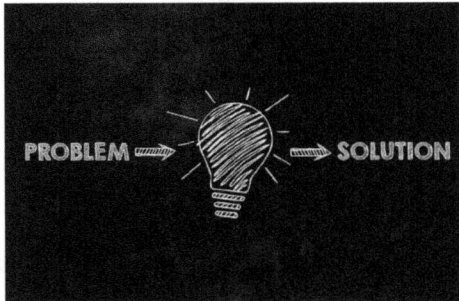

PROBLEM ➟ SOLUTION

---

[6] Margaret Reynolds, "Services, Not Products, Drive Next Wave of Growth for Manufacturers," Breakthrough Masters Unlimited, https://www.breakthroughmaster.com/2019/03/services-not-products-drive-next-wave-of-growth-for-manufacturers/.

Selling solutions is a valuable win-win with benefits for not just the customer, but the provider, too.

**Solutions have a larger impact on the customers' outcomes,** so they promote the discussion to a higher level in the organization, allowing relationships to be developed with decision-makers who have broader scope. This helps organizations escape some of the price pressure usually brought to bear by dealing with purchasing departments buying off of spec.

**Selling solutions increases loyalty when it is clear you have the customer's back,** helping them meet their goals and making them look good to the people upstairs.

**Often, solutions are much more integrated into operational planning** and involve longer-term systems, increasing longevity of the relationship. Systems aren't replaced as often as products within them.

**If your organization is in charge of the system or solution,** you have more control over the other parts or equipment used in the system and can add in more of your offering.

**If you sell the solution,** the orders for the product come with it.

How do you find out what solutions to offer or how to offer them? Market intelligence. Identify and follow the moves of strategic-driven, growth-oriented companies in any industry, like Amazon and Apple. How could you apply some of the same principles to your business? Ask customers what they are measured on and what problems they routinely have to manage that get in the way of meeting those goals. What solutions could you provide to solve them?

There are obvious services for most companies to offer.

**Training.** As baby boomers retire, sellers are losing relationships and customers are losing institutional knowledge. Providing training helps develop new advocates for a brand while providing a needed service to the customer.

**Consulting**. Having engineers or experienced tech help that can interact with customers is valuable; it not only provides insights to customers on how to maximize efficiencies or value from a product, but is also a data collection engine for the company to use in understanding customers' needs even better. This can be done as a reactive request to a customer's problem but is even better when it is offered proactively to prevent problems.

**Solutions development**. This goes beyond offering advice to offering answers. If the client's fundamental objective is greater productivity, how could they redesign their use of products or change their systems or behavior to get a better result? Most great new products are born from this kind of thinking—identify a problem, then solve it. The answer is rarely just tweaking an existing product; it usually means developing a new approach. And in this world of instant data and real time expectations, the answer usually involves services combined with products. For example, instead of just selling equipment in response to a customer's need for greater productivity, what if you also addressed floor layout of equipment, setup process speed, and inventory availability? In so doing, you might offer to provide additional equipment to help improve flow, function, and speed. You are not selling the product; you are selling the result.

Market intelligence that helps you identify gaps in the market which align with organizational strengths gives companies the confidence to think and act boldly, delivering on this first strand of GrowthDNA. It requires understanding macro market needs, then applying discernment by understanding the capabilities of the company to find the area of greatest potential growth for the organization. The intersection of where customer needs line up with a company's differentiating capabilities defines the future potential of the company.

## GROWTH OPPORTUNITY IDENTIFICATION

*The Intersection Defines the Sweet Spot of Potential*

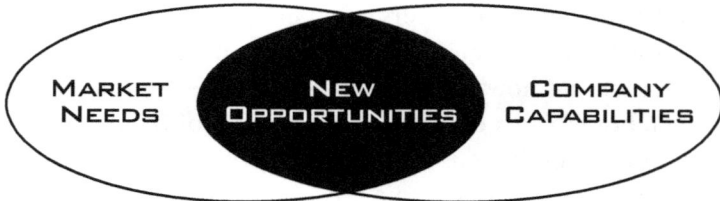

**MARKET NEEDS** — **NEW OPPORTUNITIES** — **COMPANY CAPABILITIES**

**FIGURE 4.1**

Market Intelligence boosts ConfidenceDNA because it is fact-based. Facts are not emotional or experiential. They provide a greater degree of objectivity in business decision-making, they promote alignment in understanding across different business functions, and more often than you might think, they debunk company lore. Consider how sabermetrics has changed how the sport of baseball recruits and manages offense. By defining the data that aligns with wins, the experience of baseball scouts and their historic emphasis on recruiting "five-tool" players is now trumped by algorithms.[7] The statistic that has the highest correlation with winning performance is on-base percentage, not home runs as many might expect. Great leaders use data because they understand that new insights, combined with industry knowledge, provide superior and relevant solutions—a powerful and winning combination.

Amazon is a giant in market intelligence. They excel in one-click checkout and tracking customer interests. They applied that knowledge to developing an Amazon GO store in downtown Seattle. The store is a neighborhood grocery designed to provide a cashier-free shopping experience. Just scan your phone when you enter and using Artificial Intelligence and cameras, the store records what you take off shelves. When you

---

[7] Michael Lewis, *Moneyball: the Art of Winning an Unfair Game* (New York: W.W. Norton, 2013).

are done shopping, just leave and it is automatically charged to your account. Sure, Amazon is a giant with years of experience growing through market intelligence; very few companies have their depth of market intelligence DNA. The key is to start. Start now. Start simple. Start collecting relevant data from customers and marrying that with trends. If the organization can't answer the question, "Why do customers buy from us over the alternatives?" based on what is known versus what is assumed, this is a good place to start. Decisions based on market intelligence nurture ConfidenceDNA and without it, many companies settle for incremental growth rather than defining and achieving their potential.

Your organization needs to have a market intelligence capability that allows key decision-makers throughout the company to know:

1.  What are the macro trends that will influence the market in the next three to five years?

    **Economic cycles**: Is the economy expanding or declining?

    **Technological capabilities**: What advances are being made, such as 3D printing or autonomous vehicles, that could impact every business?

    **Strategic trends**: What are the leaders in high-profile industries doing and why? How might you learn from them and apply that knowledge to your company?

    **Political and legal ramifications**: What are the potential consequences of significant changes, like in health care, compliance, or trade relations, that could rock your world?

    **Demographic and value trends**: Which generations do you market to, how is that changing, and how do the different values of each generation impact what you do and how you do it?

2.  What industry-specific trends are likely to play a role in your organization's future growth?

    **Industry concentration**: Will there be consolidation or growth?

    **Economic markets**: What are the drivers of price in your particular market?

    **Geographic implications**: What kind of shifts will occur in global or regional markets?

    **Disruptive technology**: Is your industry ripe for disruptive business models?

3.  What drivers are most likely to influence your specific company's growth, given its position in the market?

    **Customer value shifts**: What matters more to your customers than before? How are their needs changing?

    **Competitive strategy**: Are there competitive shifts that will impact your business? Are there new players testing new business models?

    **Company economics**: Where are you making and losing money? Which customers are generating the bulk of your profits?

    **Company capabilities**: What unique strengths can your company leverage?

This is by no means an exhaustive list. Your market intelligence needs are dependent upon many variables, including your industry, your potential vulnerabilities, and your growth aspirations. Being aware of outside-in information, and making decisions based on it, will encourage you to consider being the disruptor instead of just trying to mitigate the inroads of others when they introduce new products, woo customers with price reductions, or install more productive equipment. *ConfidenceDNA, the first strand of GrowthDNA, is dependent on robust, outside-in market intelligence.*

## CHAPTER SUMMARY

1. Relentless market pressure often requires the organization to take a different approach—an outside-in approach—to developing growth strategy and solving daily business problems.

2. A fast-growing trend that is adding new revenue streams to traditional manufacturers is the addition of services.

3. Market intelligence helps you identify gaps in the market that align with organizational strengths and gives companies the confidence to think and act boldly, delivering on the first strand of GrowthDNA.

4. Market intelligence should include macro, industry-specific, and company-specific data.

5. Companies with strong market intelligence make bolder decisions as they are buoyed by having indisputable facts upon which to make decisions.

6. Factual data helps align perspectives across functional areas, minimizing emotional or experiential biases.

## KEY QUESTIONS

1.  Does your organization make data-driven decisions?

2.  Do you have a robust data capture and reporting system that factors a variety of market and customer information into decision-making?

3.  Does your company regularly share data across the organization to help align knowledge and decision-making?

4.  Given the quality of the data available in your organization, do you have high confidence in decision-making?

5.  Does your data allow you to make bigger decisions without feeling they are more risky?

6.  Do you have a detailed understanding of your customers' profitability?

7.  Does your data tell you why your customers choose to buy from you over the competitors?

8.  Do you measure success at all levels of the company by meeting or exceeding metrics?

9.  Do you collect customer satisfaction information regularly?

10. Do your most valuable metrics include more than financials and operations?

## CHAPTER 5

# ClarityDNA Is Created Through Strategy

Strategy answers the question of where an organization will play in the marketplace and how it will win. It is not a list of actions, but rather a single overarching concept that guides every decision of the organization. Southwest Airlines is a low-cost leader. Apple has historically been a product innovator. These are unique strategies that describe how these organizations win. Like a compass, strategy navigates the company from today to tomorrow.

Growth strategy, the kind that enables organizations to double or quadruple in size, is not founded on incremental thinking. If you are asking how your organization can be better, you are engaging in an exercise of incremental improvement—valuable and necessary to achieve operational excellence, but not to be confused with strategy. The right question with which to lead strategy development is, "What is our potential?" It requires big ideas rooted in market knowledge. It demands letting go of what an organization has always done to embrace the potential of

> *The right question with which to lead strategy development is, "What is our potential?"*

what could be done. It doesn't start with what is being done now; instead, it defines what is needed.

Defining strategy is not enough. Strategy must be extremely clear. In order for strategy to take root in an organization and serve as a driver of performance, it must be understood by everyone involved in its implementation. Clarity of strategy is as important as the strategy itself. Leaders who share strategy without defining what it looks like in the organization are unintentionally undermining results. To be clear, leaders must define what specific changes are needed in the organization, what the new priorities will be (and equally important, what they will not be), what contributions are needed from each department and person, how success will be measured, and where new grassroot ideas and solutions are encouraged.

Clear strategy is like a funnel, with the broadest strategy decisions at the top. As each strategic decision is made, it takes options off the table for strategic decisions that follow. Strategy is a choice; by default, selecting a strategy eliminates others while creating focus. The strategic funnel consists of the following strategic decisions:

**Overarching strategy**. This is an externally oriented, high-level concept that answers the question, "How do we win in the market?" The strategic choice will not be unique to your company or even your industry, but how you implement it will be. One overarching strategy is a low-cost position. Walmart is a great example of a company with this strategy. From their advertising, which focuses on low cost, to their world-class excellence in supply chain management to reduce systemic costs, they have successfully developed a business model that allows them to make a comparable margin while charging less. Unless you are a low-cost company, you can't effectively or sustainably compete on cost. Another popular strategy is customer focus. Patagonia has developed a value system and product array that connects the company to people who value the outdoors enough to cherish it and invest in its sustainability—whether they are paying premium prices for apparel and equipment or giving charitably to eco-preserving organizations and causes. An organization must understand what needs it can best serve to make this strategic decision—knowledge that emanates from market intelligence.

**Strategic positioning**. This strategy decision determines how the organization will compete against others in the industry. It defines how the company will differentiate itself from its competitors—even those that share the same overarching strategy. How will the organization focus its energy and resources? What will it be best at? Positioning defines the go-to-market message. All too often, we see companies promise "best quality, products, and service" on their website. In other words, they claim to be best at everything. The challenge is that when every company promises the same thing, none of it matters, and companies end up competing on price. Leaders need to understand what makes their organizations unique, truly different, and invest in widening that gap between themselves and their competitors. One of the most unexpected principles of growth important to boosting ClarityDNA is the clearer the focus, the greater the growth.

> *One of the most unexpected principles of growth important to boosting ClarityDNA is the clearer the focus, the greater the growth.*

**Value proposition**. This captures the benefits a company intends to deliver to customers. What are the handful of benefits a customer derives from doing business with you over the alternatives available to them? If you are Lexus, it is customer service after the sale. If you are Amazon, it is convenience in the form of speed of delivery and the broadest range of products. A company like Patagonia is known for quality, but also for having users design the products. If you are a mountain climber, knowing that the product designer understands what it is like to be literally hanging from a hook in a rock generates expert credibility and a high standard for quality. Once defined, companies need to excel at consistently delivering against these benefits better than competitors.

**Target customers**. Regardless of which strategy you choose, not all customers seek it. Not everyone likes to shop at Walmart. Some may shop there for select goods, while others view Walmart as their go-to. For Walmart to be successful, its leaders must understand each of these types of customers and their role in the company's overall success. Walmart invests more heavily in the customers who generate the largest share of its profits and present the best opportunity for growth.

**Product/service mix**. Once an organization determines how it will compete, what benefits it provides, and who it will serve, identifying which products or services to offer is directly linked to those previous decisions. If convenience is a benefit, the organization will want to be sure to identify products and services that offer more of it than other alternatives available to the customer. See figure 5.1.

# Strategy = Clarity

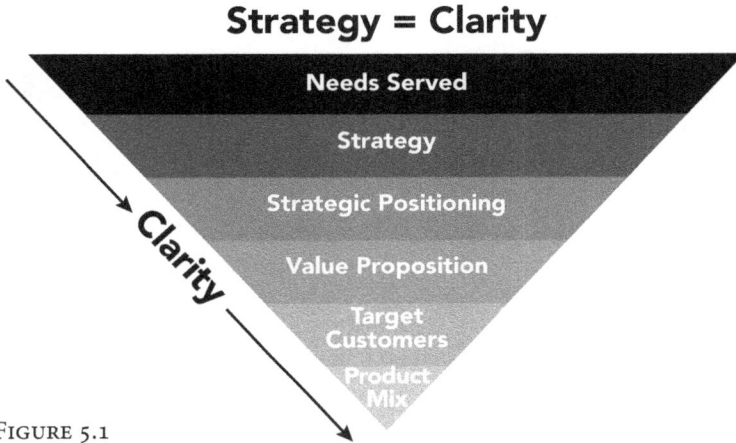

FIGURE 5.1

Strategy is different from what a company makes. Being an industry leader in widgets doesn't describe why customers buy. When what a company makes is challenged by new technology (which it eventually will be), then a strategy built on being the best widget producer becomes outdated. For instance, does Hallmark Cards make cards or sell feel-good sentiment? The former suffered with the advent of digital communication. Fortunately, over time, Hallmark has been able to adjust, and today the company has become one of the largest archives and original producers of happy stories on TV.

Apple has established that its advantage doesn't come from a specific industry or device; it doesn't just make hardware. Apple offers an innovative and user-friendly operating system that has allowed the company to make a wide variety of products, penetrate multiple industries, and adapt to the latest technology.

Connecting strategy to a specific solution rather than the underlying need jeopardizes long-term performance, tying activities to operations rather than market behavior. Good strategy can and should last for many years.

## STRATEGY IS BASED ON NEED

| Who | Fundamental Need | What They Sell |
|---|---|---|
| Amazon | Convenience | Online access to products |
| Ace Printing Company | Increase communication effectiveness | Printing |
| Hallmark Cards, Inc. | Sharing memorable moments | Greeting cards |
| Lee Jeans | Fit | Blue jeans |
| Santa Fe Railroad | Transporting goods | Railroad |
| Ford | Top personal vehicles | Model T, Ford F-150 |

FIGURE 5.2

Leaders need to continually assess the clarity of strategy. *Strategy needs to be unique to your organization, directional at an enterprise level, broad enough to encourage scalability, and specific enough to be clear.*

ClarityDNA comes from a well-defined strategy and is the essential second strand of GrowthDNA.

*Connecting strategy to a specific solution rather than the underlying need jeopardizes long-term performance, tying activities to operations rather than market behavior.*

## CHAPTER SUMMARY

1. Strategy answers the question of how an organization will win in the market.

2. The right question with which to lead strategy development is "What is our potential?"

3. Clarity of strategy is as important as the strategy itself. In order for strategy to take root in an organization and serve as a driver of performance, it must be understood by everyone involved in its implementation.

4. Clear strategy is like a funnel, with the broadest strategy decisions at the top. The following strategic decisions are included:

   a. Overarching strategy

   b. Strategic positioning

   c. Value proposition

   d. Target customer

   e. Product/Service offerings

5. Strategy is different from what a company makes; rather, it defines what impact the organization is trying to have on its customers.

6. Strategy needs to be unique to your organization, directional at an enterprise level, broad enough to encourage scalability, and specific enough to be clear.

## KEY QUESTIONS

1. Can everyone in the organization easily define the strategy?

2. When asked to describe your strategy, does everyone in the organization use the same key words or phrases?

3. Are your organization's specific capabilities a true source of advantage?

4. Does your strategy put you ahead of trends?

5. Is your strategy specific about where and how to compete?

6. Does your strategy rest on proprietary insights?

7. Is your strategy free from historical bias?

8. Does your organization have a precise definition of high-priority target customers?

9. Does your strategy anticipate how technological advances will change the market and is flexible enough to accommodate for that?

10. Is your strategy long-term in nature?

## CHAPTER 6

# CommitmentDNA Emanates From Leadership

In companies with GrowthDNA, leaders understand their role to be that of coach, not just boss. Coaches are effective at providing the game plan, or strategy, and motivating players to cross the finish line. For growth to occur, the collective brain power of the organization must be engaged. Almost any tangible advantage in business is short-lived or replicable, but people and creativity are not. Developing buy-in and encouraging contribution at an individual level is central to success. Commitment on behalf of individuals in the organization enables not only the enthusiastic embrace of the company's priorities, but also an acceptance of the responsibility to implement them.

In chapter 2, we spoke of how many strategic plans fail. Depending on which report you read, 70–90 percent fail to

∝

*It is indeed a paradox that the day-to-day operations most organizations claim as a strength undermine achieving strategic results.*

∝

return the projected value. The reason most commonly cited? Failure to execute. It is indeed a paradox that the day-to-day operations most organizations claim as a strength undermine achieving strategic results. In a *Harvard Business Review* article by Michael C. Mankins and Richard Steele, "Turning Great Strategy into Great Performance," research showed that the average realized performance of a strategic plan is 63 percent.[8] Put another way, 37 percent of anticipated performance is lost during execution. The issues with execution are common, and to an extent predictable, but also manageable.

Of all the statistics regarding the success, or rather lack of success, with strategy implementation, one commonly cited statistic bothers me more than the rest. Only one in four strategic initiatives—specific projects and programs implemented to achieve the strategy and its goals—return value. Those are unacceptable odds whether you are running a business or playing in Vegas.

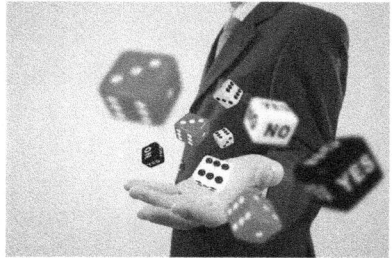

When I ask CEOs why the return on strategic growth initiatives is so low, they seem to know exactly why. They admit having experienced it themselves, and the most common reasons follow.

**Growth initiatives are not properly vetted**. Every idea is a good idea until you spend money on it and it fails to produce. In other words, ideas need to be defined more precisely before being acted on or resourced. Often, in the process of determining how the strategy will be implemented, teams will suggest and rank ideas, then move forward into budgeting and implementation. A crucial step, vetting the ideas, is missed. When my clients

---

[8] Michael C. Mankins and Richard Steele, "Turning Great Strategy into Great Performance," *Harvard Business Review*, July 2005. https://hbr.org/2005/07/turning-great-strategy-into-great-performance.

reach this stage of our work together, we use a two-page template that guides them through the investigative process: It asks questions regarding the objective or purpose, the scope, and the steps required to investigate further, as well as how to implement, the resources required, where they will come from, and potential issues they might face in implementation. Does your organization have a process of validating the potential impact of initiatives before approving them?

**There are too many projects.** One of the most common issues that gets in the way of achieving goals is too many projects. As driven leaders aspiring to be the best among our peers, we always have more things to do than money or time allow. But that doesn't always stop us from trying to sneak as much onto the list as possible. Too many initiatives are created when they are generated by functional areas rather than for the entire enterprise. Each manager wants to continue to improve his or her area—sales, operations, marketing, human resources— and there is a multiplier effect. It is not hard to reach twenty or more projects. The challenge is that many of them require the same resources for implementation, such as IT, R&D, or business development. All of the projects get compromised and sub-optimized because there just aren't adequate resources to support them all in the same time frame.

**The initiatives are not aligned with resources.** There is usually a very long list of projects that require funding over baseline departmental budgets. During budgeting time, leaders are asked to prioritize, but operational and strategic initiative funding comes from the same pot of money. The same *Harvard Business Review* article that asserted the average strategic plan returns 63 percent of its potential value cites the lack of adequate resources as the number one cause of diminished value, contributing 7.5 percent of the 37 percent loss.[9] Rather than trying to

[9] Mankins and Steele, "Turning Great Strategy into Great Performance."

accommodate everything and everyone, it is important that leaders prioritize and balance the types of projects.

With one GrowthDNA client, after leaders created the company-wide growth initiatives, other ongoing operational initiatives were added to the list. This created an overwhelming list, and while not all initiatives would drive growth, some were necessary from an operational point of view. How should they prioritize? We separated the projects by type: (1) projects done to improve operational infrastructure necessary for future growth and productivity, (2) projects that were of the highest strategic priority that deserved resource investment, (3) projects that were of strategic importance, but would be done with current resources, and (4) projects that would impact strategic results, but for which there were no available resources currently.

The projects receiving incremental resources were mostly strategic growth drivers. We limited the number of short-term operational initiatives to those that would have significant company-wide impact and support the new strategic direction. The rationale was that many operational issues would be addressed (reduced or eliminated) through greater strategic focus and shared initiatives, which creates alignment throughout the organization; what remained could be dealt with on a case-by-case basis. The last group would be re-prioritized as resources allowed.

The key here is to not let urgency be the primary driver: Impact, or how far and how fast the initiative advances the business toward its potential, should be.

What strengthens the genetic conformation of Commitment-DNA?

**Strategic growth initiatives are identified at the company, not department, level**. If organizations started with a clear strategic vision of the future and generated initiatives at the company level, asking each department what they must do to support those initiatives, there would be fewer total initiatives, more cross-company synergy, and a cleaner allocation of resources, with less overload and backlog.

**Limit the total number of initiatives in a given time frame.** The challenges of project overload are many, and you probably know them well. Trying to do too many things with too few resources means few things work; a lot of effort for little gain. It is much more effective to do fewer, bigger things really well with clear resource prioritization. Typically, results are much more significant—the kind of impact that can move the needle.

**Reward employees for results, not activities.** As we engage employees in high-profile growth initiatives, we need to be sure we are not rewarding projects and people for activities completed, but rather for results achieved. Department managers need to be trained to think about how their roles support the company agenda rather than focusing on their department operations in a vacuum. All employees should understand what the company priorities are so they can give that work the attention it deserves.

**Properly allocate and align resources with priorities.** Reallocating resources that feel scarce to begin with is a challenge most organizations face. It is even worse for those organizations in mature or declining industries that feel the pressure of decreasing revenue and margins. Often overlooked is the fact that, while priorities need to be funded, the strategy in place is a choice and dictates what doesn't fit. It is probable that practices, products, or procedures currently in place can be eliminated as they no longer fit the direction of the new organization. While the concept is usually easy to grasp, its implementation requires significant discipline.

**Communication cannot be overrated.** The same *Harvard Business Review* study referenced previously revealed that the majority of unrealized growth potential is largely the result, not of market factors or external influences, but of poor communication.[10] That includes things like poorly communicated strategy, activities not clearly defined, unclear accountabilities, organizational silos, and inadequate performance monitoring. Nothing is more important to the successful implementation of growth initiatives than ongoing, consistent, and visible communication about the strategy, its priorities, and progress on both.

## SOURCES OF THIRTY-SEVEN PERCENT PERFORMANCE LOSS

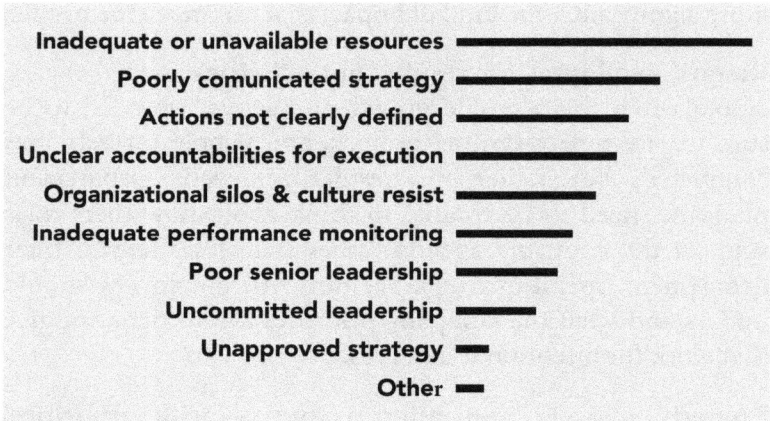

Inadequate or unavailable resources ━━━━━━━━━━━
Poorly comunicated strategy ━━━━━━━━━
Actions not clearly defined ━━━━━━━
Unclear accountabilities for execution ━━━━━━
Organizational silos & culture resist ━━━━━
Inadequate performance monitoring ━━━━
Poor senior leadership ━━━
Uncommitted leadership ━━
Unapproved strategy ━
Other ━

FIGURE 6.1

Any organization that doesn't have a purposeful, proactive communication plan, faithfully implemented, is vulnerable to the employee malaise that comes from being lulled into doing what they are told rather than inspired to create value. Committed organizations are enthusiastic, proactive, and grassroots innovators. Only leadership has the authority and influence to determine the direction of the company and to prioritize investment. It is leadership who must convey and convince the stakeholders essential for successful

---

[10] Mankins and Steele, "Turning Great Strategy into Great Performance."

implementation to get on board with the direction of the organization. To do so, leadership must be able to communicate not only the importance of the strategy to the company, but also, more importantly, to its employees—collectively and individually. Not until leaders feel they are "broken records," spending far too much time communicating the same critical message, have they likely started achieving traction.

Kevin Brown, CEO of Omaha Steel, a company with 42 percent growth in 2017, sums it up. "Most of my focus over the last ten months compared to three years ago is on employee communication. We all try to roll up our sleeves to get the job done. When people see your heart, that you are willing to work alongside them, and know your interests are in the right spot, it is amazing to see what people will do for each other. We are rowing the boat together. For us to continue to move forward, the only thing that will stop us is us. We need to be sure the team stays fully vested in wanting success. The rest of it solves itself."

Great leaders drive commitment by communicating unceasingly and engaging people in solutions. *Developing Commitment-DNA in all stakeholders so that all can contribute to performance, as measured by outcomes not activities, is the third strand of GrowthDNA.*

> *Great leaders drive commitment by communicating unceasingly and engaging people in solutions.*

## CHAPTER SUMMARY

1. GrowthDNA leaders need to be coaches and encourage employees to get in the game. Developing buy-in and encouraging contribution at an individual level is central to success.

2. When growth plans fail, it is usually due to poor execution. Those organizations that succeed still lose, on average, 37 percent of projected value associated with strategic plans.

3. Only one of every four strategic growth initiatives return value. The most common reasons are:

   a. Initiatives are not fully vetted.

   b. The impact on human capital resources is not considered.

   c. Priority projects don't receive adequate funding.

4. To increase the odds of successful growth results:

   a. Identify strategic initiatives on company level, not department level.

   b. Limit the number of total high-priority initiatives in a given time frame.

   c. Reward employees for results, not activities.

   d. Allocate appropriate resources for project success.

   e. Communicate priorities clearly, consistently, and visibly.

## KEY QUESTIONS

1. Are the action steps required to successfully implement the strategy well defined?

2. Are resources allocated in a manner consistent with the strategic priorities?

3. Does everyone in the organization understand how to contribute to strategic success?

4. Does the strategy forecast profitable growth at a rate exceeding the industry growth average?

5. Do you have and use metrics that provide an early indication of strategic success?

6. Are your interim metrics effective leading indicators of year-end financial performance?

7. Is the strategic direction clearly communicated to all in the organization regularly?

8. Has a communication plan for ongoing strategic communication been developed?

9. Is there a commitment to strategic implementation throughout the organization at all levels?

10. Is there an effective tool or method for updating employees on strategic implementation progress?

## CHAPTER 7

# CultureDNA Drives Performance

The final DNA strand, and perhaps the most critical because it drives sustainability, is culture. Culture is the collection of behaviors—derived from shared attitudes, values, goals, and practices—that characterize an institution or organization. Every organization has a culture—some by default, and some that are purposefully created. Cultures that seek to maximize a department or function, rather than thinking about how that function can contribute to the success of the overall organization, detract from long-term growth. This promotes an incremental approach to improvement and contributes to organizational silos. The Gallup organization reminds us every couple of years that nearly 70 percent of employees are disengaged.[11] According to Deloitte, 94 percent of executives believe that a distinctive culture is connected to success, but fewer than one in three executives (28 percent) report that they understand their organization's culture.[12] *Forbes* shares that companies with strong cultures saw a 400 percent increase in revenue growth.[13]

---

[11] Jim Harter, "Employee Engagement on the Rise in the U.S." Gallup.com, November 21, 2018. https://news.gallup.com/poll/241649/employeeengagement-rise.aspx.

[12] "Culture of Purpose-Building business confidence; driving growth, 2014 core beliefs and culture survey." Deloitte.com, 2014. https://www2.deloitte.com/content/dam/Deloitte/us/Documents/aboutdeloitte/us-leadership-2014-core-beliefs-culture-survey-040414.pdf.

[13] Kotter, John, "Does Corporate Culture Drive Financial Performance?" *Forbes*. Forbes Magazine, June 23, 2012. https://www.forbes.com/sites/johnkotter/2011/02/10/does-corporate-culture-drive-financial-performance/#5898bf507e9e.

An effective culture has to be established at the top of the house. GrowthDNA companies have a growth-minded culture. In addition to having specified important values that define company culture, behaviors that support growth are expected at all levels of the company.

What does a growth-minded culture look like?

**Aligned.** Leaders and managers across all functional areas must be aligned by common objectives and priorities. Changing culture starts with changing the leadership approach. Department leaders need to be rewarded based on overall company performance, not departmental excellence alone. Furthermore, the leadership team must function as an integrated team, working together to achieve high-priority projects that foster growth—no silos allowed. Leaders and managers can't cultivate an involved culture if they themselves are not clear about strategy, priorities, and decision-making parameters.

**Transparent.** Everyone in the organization must understand the direction of the company or its vision. As Lewis Carroll in *Alice in Wonderland* reminds us, "If you don't know where you are going, any road will get you there."[14]

Companies without clear direction are always chasing the next shiny thing. Companies with clear direction are able to communicate how every employee can support the strategy. One company I have worked with asks each and every employee,

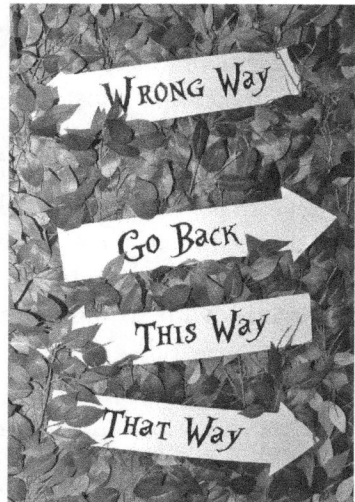

---

[14] Lewis Carroll, *Alice's Adventures in Wonderland*. Church Hanborough, Oxford: Artists' Choice Editions, 2009.

regardless of their role, to report three ways he or she has sup-ported the strategy, every quarter, as part of the performance management system. Initially, what the employee has done is less important than developing the habit of thinking about how those actions impact the company as a whole. Over time, the action items become more meaningful.

**Strategic specificity.** How the organization plans to achieve its vision must be clear. This includes the critical choices made in the strategic funnel (see chapter 5)—the overarching strategy, how it will compete in the market, the benefits the organization will consistently provide to customers that help distinguish it further, the target customers it prioritizes, and the products and services that those customers value. Think about a new employee working the production line that reads in an employee manual that the organization values quality. Chances are they won't do their job differently unless they understand what the company means by quality—is it precision, cleanliness, functionality, or all of the above? Do they understand how they contribute to that quality? Do they know what to do if what they are working on is questionable? Employees can't help if they don't know what is expected and what they are empowered to do.

**Clear priorities.** The company priorities must be defined. Ideally, they should be ranked. Be as explicit as possible. It helps employees plan how to allocate their time, but it also gives them information about opportunities that they can volunteer to support, over their regular duties, adding more value to the company and strengthening their career prospects. A growth-minded culture looks for ways to engage employees beyond their day-to-day routine.

**Informed.** ClarityDNA goes beyond telling employees what the direction of the company is; it requires employees to understand how to contribute. Employees must understand what results the company expects and how they are doing against those goals. Everyone in the company wins when goals are met, so understanding what they are and how to contribute to them is important. This isn't limited to financial metrics. It includes understanding who the target customer is, how well they are being served, and how they could be served better. It means they need to understand the state of the market so they know what is helping and hurting the company's growth and think about potential solutions. And yes, they need to understand how their choices and decisions in their daily work impacts the company's financial results.

**Diffused decision-making.** Decisions should occur at all levels of the organization. All decision makers at every level need to have insight into the company's criteria used for investing in new solutions so they can make thoughtful recommendations, enabling decision-making authority to be dispersed. If all decisions are made in the board room, executives have set themselves up as a bottleneck. Organizations with strong growth-minded cultures empower and enable appropriate decisions at all levels of the organization. To effectively empower employees, they must have knowledge. All managers should be training employees to be knowledgeable in four key areas: financial performance and what makes it tick; strategy or direction of the company and what it prioritizes; the market variables that impact

*If all decisions are made in the board room, executives have set themselves up as a bottleneck. Organizations with strong growth-minded cultures empower and enable appropriate decisions at all levels of the organization.*

success like customers' needs and wants the company is trying to serve, as well as who key customers are; and operational implications up and down stream of their work so they know how their decisions will impact others. If we expect accountability, we must educate employees so they can have some say in their work.

**Inclusive.** Employees are encouraged to contribute ideas and solutions not just identify problems. As leaders, we often succumb to time pressures and find that telling employees how to solve a problem seems most expedient. The alternative, to educate them to solve the problem themselves, just takes too long. Yet, as time-starved managers, we put ourselves in a no-win situation. We stunt their growth and add to our own workload. To change that takes time and an "ask, don't tell" approach. When they bring you a problem, you ask them how they would solve it. If they aren't sure, you coach them and help them figure out what they need to learn in order to do so. Point them in the right direction, but don't do it for them. In a few months, your operating bandwidth as a functional unit will increase geometrically with no increase in headcount. Without it, you manage employees who either don't know how to think creatively or don't feel welcome to.

In *Turn the Ship Around*, David Marquet, retired Naval captain, shares insights about how to engage people and improve performance.[15] Recognizing the power of teamwork and determined to generate more leadership than followership, he challenges traditional leadership practices. Some examples include: Having conversations instead of having meetings, focusing on people over technology, augmenting direction with rich, contextual, informal communication, and giving control rather than taking it.

---

[15] Lt. David Marquet, *Turn the Ship Around! How to Create Leadership at Every Level* (Austin, TX: Greenleaf Book Group Press, 2012).

**Active communicators.** Communication needs to be a two-way street. It is not sufficient for leadership to communicate vision and priorities. It is essential that employees understand and are inspired by what lies ahead. Far too often the communication fails to answer *why* a decision has been made. Without the why, employees can't learn, and they are probably less likely to be motivated to change just because someone said so. Those closest to the front lines are essential in the smooth implementation of new initiatives. Growth initiatives created in the board room are not implemented there. Employees can help executives execute them better and more effectively if they have a voice in the process. Leaders also need to listen for understanding. Has communication been clear enough? You will know the answer is yes, when employees start using the same words and phrases knowledgably to describe their company and its priorities.

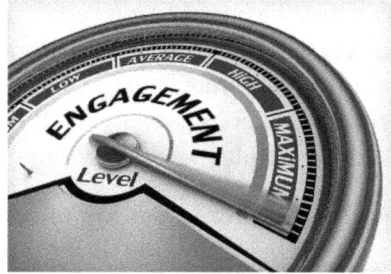

>  ✕
> *Growth initiatives created in the board room are not implemented there.*
> ✕

While these are some of the common tenets of a growth-minded culture, the solution is different for every organization because they each start in a different place, have different values, and different long-term goals. The keys to a growth-minded culture are awareness of what is needed, communication that motivates action, and accountability for all to drive results. Often, that means new processes are needed to educate and empower employees while rewarding outcomes, not actions. The fourth strand, a growth-minded culture, generating engaged and empowered employees, is essential for achieving and especially sustaining next-stage business growth.

∝

*The keys to a growth-minded culture are awareness of what is needed, communication that motivates action, and accountability for all to drive results.*

∝

## CHAPTER SUMMARY

1. CultureDNA is critical as it drives sustainability.

2. Culture is the collection of behaviors of an organization—derived from shared attitudes, values, goals, and practices—that characterize an institution or organization.

3. A strong culture can have a dramatic impact on the performance of an organization. The Gallup organization states that nearly 70 percent of employees are actively disengaged. According to Deloitte, 94 percent of executives believe that a distinctive culture is connected to success but fewer than one in three executives (28 percent) report that they understand their organization's culture. Forbes shares that companies with strong cultures saw a 400 percent increase in revenue growth.

4. GrowthDNA companies have a growth-minded culture. Characteristics of this culture include:

    a. **Alignment** across functional areas and effective teamwork at all levels of the organization.

    b. **Transparent** understanding of the key components of strategy and the growth plan across all levels of the organization, not just leadership.

    c. **Strategic specificity** that ensures all stakeholders understand how the strategy impacts their role.

    d. **Clear priorities** linked to resource allocation guide investment and day-to-day work.

e. **Informed** employees that understand the current performance of the business.

f. **Dispersed decision-making** means employees are training to solve problems and to do so they must understand the strategy, financial performance, marketing trends, and operational processes.

g. **Inclusiveness** encourages employees to contribute ideas and solutions not just identify problems.

h. **Active communication,** which includes two-way communication, is the norm.

5. The keys to a growth-minded culture are awareness of what is needed, communication that motivates action, and accountability for all to drive results.

## KEY QUESTIONS

1. Has the strategy been clearly communicated to all employees?

2. Does the process of strategic execution enable and encourage participation at the individual level?

3. Does the strategy influence how employees do their work every day?

4. Do employees understand the key criteria used in making strategic decisions?

5. Is decision-making dispersed throughout the organization rather than concentrated at the leadership level?

6. Does the organization regularly celebrate wins?

7. Are employees rewarded on results more than activities?

8. Does your company deploy "outside-in" thinking— or market-driven thinking—at all levels?

9. Is there sufficient bench strength for leadership positions?

10. Does strategy guide daily operational decisions?

# How GrowthDNA Works

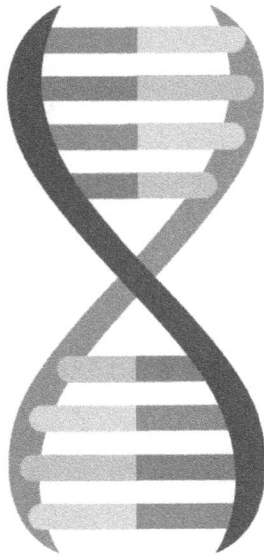

## CHAPTER 8

# Maximizing GrowthDNA Results

Human DNA information is essentially stored as a code of four chemical bases: adenine (A), guanine (G), cytosine (C), and thymine (T). There are about three billion bases, and more than 99 percent of those bases are the same in all people.[16] *The order, or sequence, of these bases determines the information available for building and maintaining an organism, similar to the way in which letters of the alphabet appear in a certain order to form words and sentences.*

In GrowthDNA, every organization has the same four strands—ConfidenceDNA, ClarityDNA, CommitmentDNA, and CultureDNA. As with human DNA, sequence matters.

Equally important is the degree of presence, or level, of each strand. Human DNA can be modified.[17] While the sequence of DNA may not be affected by your environment, the way genes work—called gene expression—can. *Epigenetics* is the study of heritable changes in gene expression that don't involve changing the underlying DNA—effectively, software changes that cause alterations in gene function. This can occur either through natural causes or through genetic manipulation. So too, can GrowthDNA be boosted, made stronger, to enable better outcomes.

---

[16] "What Is DNA?" U.S. National Library of Medicine (National Institutes of Health), https://ghr.nlm.nih.gov/primer/basics/dna.

[17] "DNA and Mutations," Understanding Evolution (University of California Museum of Paleontology), https://evolution.berkeley.edu/evolibrary/article/mutations_01.

Each of the four strands of GrowthDNA are essential in driving substantial and sustainable growth. These strands are intertwined and mutually reinforcing. Boosting one—say, increasing ConfidenceDNA—has a positive impact on ClarityDNA, because it enables the leadership team to make more focused choices; on CommitmentDNA, because leaders have the evidence they need to create the business case that convinces others this is the best course of action; and on CultureDNA, as knowing data encourages people to speak up and contribute. Best performance outcomes occur when all four strands are strong and are functioning interdependently. Therefore, it is important to understand how they work together.

The strands interconnect in three specific ways.

**They are cyclical.** The framework itself is dynamic, and any of the strands can be nurtured independently—just as you could treat a specific ailment in one part of the body. However, for overall health, all of your body mechanics are working at their best when the body functions are in balance physically, nutritionally, and metabolically. The same is true for GrowthDNA. To maximize overall performance, all four strands need to be strong. That said, there is a natural starting sequence for engaging with GrowthDNA at the outset. To maximize results from the first cycle, start with market intelligence. ConfidenceDNA is the foundation for all the decisions to come. After an organization finishes the first cycle, it operates much like a flywheel, as the cycle never ends. Organizations continue to grow and strengthen these strands over time. The better each gets, the more value organizations achieve, and the more value derived from each strand, the more organizations seek to boost them.

**They are cumulative.** Each strand builds on the one before it. It is impossible to have ClarityDNA without the keen insights from market intelligence that breed ConfidenceDNA; leaders won't want to narrow their focus if they are uncertain. If leaders can't clearly define their strategy, CommitmentDNA is hard to achieve. And without a clear sense of shared goals, CultureDNA is usually managed at a departmental rather than a company level. As one strand gets built out, it enables the others to be strengthened.

**They are diagnostic.** Most organizations never know why they are less successful than they expect to be. They have identified opportunities. Their teams have worked hard. What is getting in the way? It is not the activities in play, but how they are being implemented. GrowthDNA helps leaders understand which strands need work and are getting in the way of maximum function in the organization. Like human DNA, GrowthDNA is invisible and lies below the surface. It must be diagnosed in order to be understood.

> *Like human DNA, GrowthDNA is invisible and lies below the surface.*

A good friend of mine went to doctor after doctor trying to get her strange symptoms diagnosed—she was fatigued with random headaches and muscle aches. This went on for a few years before anyone put the pieces together. She has Lyme disease. Although functioning well today, she lost almost a decade to this disease. Diagnosis is the first step in treatment, and an important one. GrowthDNA can shed light on what has stymied growth in your organization, possibly for years.

## CHAPTER SUMMARY

1. The sequence of GrowthDNA matters, as it impacts the outcome, much like the order of letters create a word. Furthermore, DNA—human and business—can be genetically modified to achieve a different, better outcome.

2. Best outcomes occur when all four DNA strands are strong and functioning interdependently.

3. The strands—ConfidenceDNA, ClarityDNA, CommitmentDNA, and CultureDNA—interconnect in three ways:

   a. **They are cyclical:** There is a logical starting point and the cycle never ends.

   b. **They are cumulative:** Each strand builds on the one before.

   c. **They are diagnostic:** They provide the ability to diagnose the root cause of issues that limit growth.

## KEY QUESTIONS

1. Does your organization struggle to get the return it expects from its growth investments?

2. Does your organization feel like employees aren't as engaged as they need to be?

3. Which of the four strands do you think creates your biggest challenge?

CHAPTER 9

# GrowthDNA Is Cyclical

The initial engagement point for those wanting to boost GrowthDNA is ConfidenceDNA. Without it, other actions around the circle are typically more incremental in nature, with less impact, and often under-resourced. Leaders without confidence may have too many irons in the fire or limit resources, as they are uncertain about what to invest in and fear overinvesting. What high-growth leaders understand is that the right data helps mitigate risk by providing greater certainty that decisions and resulting actions are on the right track. Good data inspires bigger, bolder moves that can lead the industry instead of mimicking others.

Interestingly, most leaders start with commitment. In CommitmentDNA, operational execution is challenged, scoped, and defined. Without ConfidenceDNA, commitment is where the comfort zone lies for leaders who were raised in a particular function like finance or sales. They ask the question, "How can we be better?" Without realizing it, leaders are asking a question that will perpetuate the status quo. Why? Because the word *better* implies that the current business model—markets, customers, and products—is on track, and the focus becomes fixed on how to improve it, not whether to challenge or change it. That scope and view establishes limitations from the outset.

If the question asked is, "How do we make our existing product better," the solution is most likely to produce a product extension, like adding whitening formula to toothpaste. But what if what is needed is a new way of offering toothpaste—say, a variety of options, depending on circumstances, like freshening breath on date night, or whitening teeth before that vacation, or improving sensitivity before eating cold foods? What if you didn't have to buy a whole tube of toothpaste and make a choice about what to use? What if you could have a Keurig-like dispenser for the right toothpaste at the right time? Pop in the cup for the right toothpaste for today.

Does that come from asking what can we do better? Or does it come from collecting market intelligence about what is valued by customers, defining the problems customers want to solve, and the confidence to develop new approaches to the market to do it?

Key decisions are only as good as their inputs. If those inputs are timely and relevant data points that represent the needs of the market served, chances of improving performance are greater. The alternative (followed due to lack of data that inspires ConfidenceDNA) is to continue on the same path, and often, to emulate the competition (who probably doesn't have data either), or alternatively, to guess based on anecdotal evidence. You may have heard it said that hope is not a plan. The right time to invest in data is before key decisions—such as strategy— are made.

> *Key decisions are only as good as their inputs.*

Most organizations tend to have more internal data in operational and financial areas than external market intelligence. They know more about what exists inside their own four walls than what is going on in the market they are trying to serve. There is greater emphasis on cost containment, which is controllable, than market growth, which feels less certain. Information about customers, their needs, their profitability, their view of competitors, and general market trends and conditions enables leaders to think about solving customer problems rather than selling products to customers. One approach is outside-in; the other inside-out. Outside-in means looking at the company just as those outside of it—customers, competitors, or market analysts/investors— would. What do they see? It also means looking at the market with fresh eyes, unrestrained by operational legacy. What are you doing that gets in your own way?

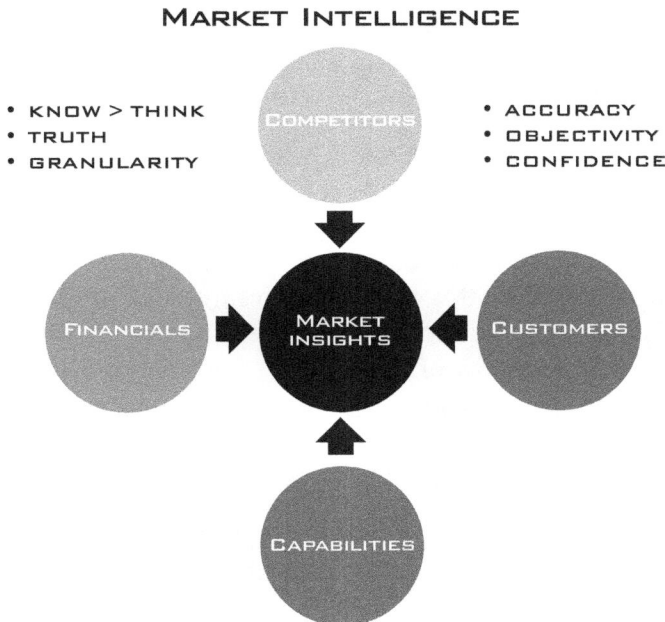

## MARKET INTELLIGENCE

- KNOW > THINK
- TRUTH
- GRANULARITY

- ACCURACY
- OBJECTIVITY
- CONFIDENCE

COMPETITORS

FINANCIALS ▶ MARKET INSIGHTS ◀ CUSTOMERS

CAPABILITIES

**FIGURE 9.1**

Plastic Enterprises is an injection-molding plastic manufacturer. It was founded in 1965 and makes round molded plastic lids for packaging of food products, serving customers that are household names in the food industry. They were plagued with a common challenge: A small number of customers accounted for a relatively large proportion of volume, and thus had control in negotiations. They were a relatively small player in a market where the top ten companies accounted for one-third of the industry, and 2,500 injection molders competed for the other two-thirds. Margin pressure was high, and they could lose business fairly easily if a competitor was willing to take the project at little to no margin—and as you know, there are always those that will.

There was a change in leadership and Plastic Enterprises was run by a new team who aspired to higher growth. They had a vision to *double* the company's growth in five years or less. It would be a challenge; this was a different trajectory than the company had been following and would require enterprise-wide change.

The new leaders brought me in when they were considering switching out the manufacturing floor from injection molding to thermoforming, a different process gaining favor in the industry. Injection molding, the current process, involves feeding material (in this case, plastic resin) into a heated barrel and forcing it into a mold cavity, where it cools and hardens to the configuration of the cavity. The change they were considering would require significant recapitalization, and it was unclear what impact it would have on the customer base or which new customers could be targeted with this technology.

As more information was gathered about the company and the market it served, it became apparent that little data existed on customers, sales patterns, and potential technology applications. Given that the GrowthDNA framework emphasizes outside-in data discovery, one of the first things I did was walk through the grocery store to discover what end customers see on the shelves, which drives behaviors and preferences of the manufacturers who are their customers. This was something they had not done for quite some time and it revealed some very interesting insights. Here was the key one: There were many round packages in an aisle they had previously dabbled in, but were currently not serving—dairy. If they were able to penetrate this market segment with existing technology, it would present an alternative to changing manufacturing processes.

After considerable debate and development of alternative case studies, the company made the decision not to pursue thermoforming, but to stick with what they knew and focus on a segment that they had previously served in a limited capacity: the dairy market. This approach would require hiring an experienced salesperson to penetrate those customers, but they believed that they could pursue this market aggressively with current production capability and capacity and focus on high-growth segments (yogurt and ice cream) in an otherwise slow-growing industry.

Along with other key business changes, the strategy paid off. Within three years of developing their growth strategy, they were building a new warehouse to accommodate the increased business. They paid down debt substantially within two years. They had experienced a significant turnaround in revenue and profit.

Without outside-in thinking, this company would have invested millions in new production processes. Instead, because of seeing the market through the end customer's lens, they were able to invest six figures in acquiring new talent and developing new approaches to their existing market. They doubled the business and spent much less.

The issue is the same for many of us: We don't know what we don't know. Isn't it time to find out?

As the organization works through the entire cycle and better understands the value of the data and how to deploy the data in decision-making, the more support there is for identification and development of data-capture and -analysis systems. This function will get more robust over time as the cycle continues and ConfidenceDNA is strengthened further. This is true of all the strands—GrowthDNA builds over time.

Organizations with strong ConfidenceDNA have an ongoing mechanism for data collection, dissemination, and decision-making. While each decision should be data-driven, a market intelligence system is something that can be built over time; thus, the concept of a cycle. It doesn't have to start as a large effort. It just has to start.

The timing of the cycle most often corresponds with an organization's natural planning cycle. However, unlike most strategic planning, it is not event- or process-driven; rather, it is dynamic and driven by the strategic issues and opportunities an organization is facing. For example, the first time through the cycle may be driven by a specific catalyst, such as lack of growth, loss of a major customer, or even the desire to create a strategic plan. That catalyst will determine what data is most needed initially. (See chapter 4 for suggestions for the type of data many companies require.) After that first cycle is completed, as progress against goals is monitored, leaders may choose to further strengthen each DNA strand as they identify other data they would like to have to build confidence, determine what further clarity is required, establish deeper organizational commitment, or define other behavioral changes that are needed for a growth-minded culture. The more experience an organization has going through the cycle, the more they strengthen each strand; the better they get, the greater value derived.

*Organizations with strong ConfidenceDNA have an ongoing mechanism for data collection, dissemination, and decision-making.*

After boosting ConfidenceDNA born of market intelligence, the organization is ready to challenge themselves to provide the ClarityDNA that comes from charting the path of growth for the organization. To accomplish that, we must ask, "What level of growth is possible for this organization to achieve?" as opposed to "What makes us better? or "What is the most probable path for us?" Possibilities capture potential, while probabilities yield predictable outcomes that are extensions of the past.

> *Possibilities capture potential, while probabilities yield predictable outcomes that are extensions of the past.*

The latter tends to lead to operational improvements within a current business model. The former frees up thinking to pursue dramatic change when paired with the confidence of market intelligence. It is a common self-limiting belief that 10× growth is not in the cards, and the company should be thrilled with a 10 percent increase. In fact, the case can be made that 10 percent may be harder to achieve than 10×.

When we think of 10 percent increases, we try to stretch what already exists in product, distribution, and resources to get there. When 10× is the goal, the organization understands things will have to be dramatically different—maybe the core business becomes one of several divisions; a local company goes global; products are sold across multiple markets rather than one, etc. New possibilities open themselves up when not restrained by the past. One question may improve the company; the other transforms it. What would 10x look like for your organization? Do you believe it is attainable? Why or why not? What holds you back?

Remember that boosting DNA can change the trajectory of your business. It leads you to new ways of thinking, the discovery of new opportunities, and new growth-oriented behaviors. Our biggest limitations are often our own beliefs in what is possible.

Strategy sets the course for the future vision of the organization. It answers the questions, "Where will we play?" and "How we will win?" As can be seen from the chart following, while understanding the market in which the organization operates is the first step (and the biggest box), all other decisions in a company are subordinate to the strategy. It is impossible to know where to

*Strategy must be directional, not theoretical; it must be specific, not general; and it must be actionable.*

invest, who to hire, or how to go to market without understanding strategy. Every person in the organization required to make decisions needs to understand the direction of the company so they can align their work to it. That is why clarity matters. Having a direction is not enough. It must be clearly understood. Strategy must be directional, not theoretical; it must be specific, not general; and it must be actionable.

### THE ENTERPRISE MODEL

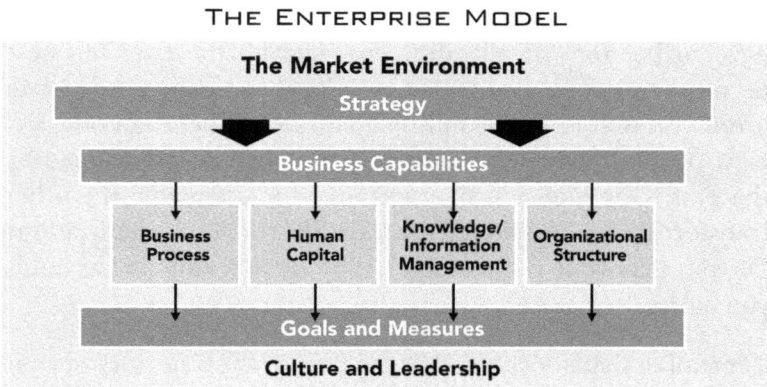

**The Market Environment**

Strategy

Business Capabilities

Business Process | Human Capital | Knowledge/Information Management | Organizational Structure

Goals and Measures

Culture and Leadership

FIGURE 9.2

Why is clarity so hard to achieve? Getting agreement is easier when the concept is vague and each person can interpret it the way he or she likes. More specific direction feels like greater risk if you lack appropriate market intelligence. It is not enough to say we have the best products, the greatest value, or the most satisfied customers. Those statements provide no direction and don't define what attributes contribute to being best, so most employees don't know what to improve. While it may feel counterintuitive, the truth is that the pace of acceleration of business growth is directly correlated to the clarity of the strategic concept that drives it.

After establishing a clear focus, leadership can begin to drive CommitmentDNA. They have a common understanding of where the organization is going and the ConfidenceDNA to commit—resources, money, and time. It is in this stage that the rest of the company needs to be brought on board. This step involves mobilizing the collective brain trust. Strategy can be created at the top of the house, but cannot be implemented there. For a company to have high-growth performance, they must engage the entire workforce with clear expectations and assignments, spawning a new energy and enthusiasm for producing value. The leadership team is responsible for providing that constant and relentless drumbeat that motivates the rest of the organization.

> *It is CommitmentDNA where value is won or lost.*

It is CommitmentDNA where value will be won or lost. Organizations that publish their vision and goals and then go back to their offices and resume doing what they did yesterday don't win. Leaders must spend a significant amount of time defining what needs to be done differently—specific programs, tasks, timelines, resource allocation, and measures to be achieved—to educate and engage employees. Furthermore, this work cannot happen in silos.

If each functional or department leader is assigned this task independently of the others, the opportunity for significant change is lost. All a leader can typically do at that point is maximize his or her own department's function within the confines of current macro systems and resources. (See chapter 6 for more details).

To boost GrowthDNA, it is imperative that leaders determine how their functional area contributes to achieving the organization's strategy rather than maximize department performance. For example, if quality is a competitive advantage, enhancing operational efficiency isn't adding value if it compromises the ability to deliver high-quality products. Investing heavy R&D in developing a bells-and-whistles gadget doesn't fit the strategy of an organization pursuing price-sensitive customers. Each senior leader, rather than being responsible for maximizing their department performance, must ask and answer the question, "How can our work maximize the performance of the company?" (A good test to use is whether priorities are so clear across the organization that there are no disputes during the budget process.)

How senior leaders behave, what and how often they communicate, and their ability to encourage two-way dialogue about the direction of the company will help strengthen the growth genetic code of CommitmentDNA.

Once leadership has been successful in communicating the strategy with clarity and developing commitment through the collective brain trust, it is time to look at how to sustain the results that company-wide programs generate by improving CultureDNA. It is not uncommon to see an initial uptick in revenue only to have it settle again at historic levels once the "phase" passes. Many longer-term employees call this the "flavor-of-the-month" or "shiny thing" syndrome.

Sustaining high performance over time requires a growth mindset to permeate the organization. This high-growth culture incorporates new ways to work, new ways to make decisions, and new ways to communicate. It knits the organization closer together while demanding more of each employee in terms of problem solving, creativity, and value contribution.

CultureDNA may be the most challenging of all the strands. It requires leaders to operate in a constant state of consciousness to avoid falling into hereditary habits. One of the biggest areas where cultures regress is believing that the answers to business challenges should be known, given the depth of experience with the category. But in fact, past knowledge is suspect if it isn't from the end customer—and their needs and expectations are constantly evolving. Admitting you don't know (without new market intelligence) after years of industry experience is a humbling act, yet absolutely necessary for future success.

For the new culture to take root, there must be a conscious effort not to make the typical decision in the normal way, but rather to always ask what does the (outside-in) data say, and what will move us the furthest the fastest toward realizing our potential and desired future state? In other words, make the decision from where you want to be, not where you are today.

> *Make the decision from where you want to be, not where you are today.*

No company is perfect, and it is not leadership's job to protect employees from mistakes or internal disagreements or vice-versa. Leaders need to be open to hearing bad news, diverse opinions, and what isn't working, just as employees do. It is in this open exchange of information that new, transformative ideas are often discovered.

If an organization wants to maximize the speed and extent of its growth, it requires every employee making value-adding contributions. That means that employees have to feel empowered and encouraged to make decisions that improve company performance. In creating that type of environment, leaders multiply the bandwidth of what can be accomplished. Leaders end up with more time to focus on the issues that only they can address, which in turn powers up the strategic growth opportunities of the company.

*If an organization wants to maximize the speed and extent of its growth, it requires every employee making value-adding contributions.*

How do you empower employees? Implement the "ask, don't tell" approach covered in chapter 7. Too often, business executives tell employees what to do. It is faster and easier than taking the time to develop employees. But this approach does nothing to develop a growth mindset. Training leaders to ask employees what they think should be done (rather than to provide answers) gives leaders the opportunity to hear new ideas while coaching employees on strategic, financial, market, or operational inputs important to the decision; a true win-win.

Once a company has examined and boosted each GrowthDNA strand, in this order, it will naturally evolve into looking at the four strands as integrated, rather than sequential, as the degree of interdependency will be better understood. Improvements in any one strand enable improved performance in the other strands.

## CHAPTER SUMMARY

1.  The initial engagement point for those wanting to build GrowthDNA is ConfidenceDNA. Without it, other actions around the circle are typically more incremental in nature, with less impact, and are often under-resourced.

2.  Most leaders attempting to drive improved performance mistakenly start with CommitmentDNA. It is in this phase that operational execution is challenged, scoped, and defined. They ask the question, "How can we be better?" instead of the more growth-oriented question, "What is our potential?"

3.  Outside-in means looking at the company just as those outside of it—customers, competitors, or market analysts/investors—would. It also means looking at the market with fresh eyes, unrestrained by internal operational legacy.

4.  As the organization works through the entire cycle, better understanding the value of the data and how to deploy the data in decision-making, more support builds for identification and development of data-capture and -analysis systems. And that is true of all the strands—GrowthDNA builds over time.

5.  It is a common self-limiting belief that 10× is not in the cards and the company should be thrilled with a 10 percent increase. In fact, the case can be made that 10 percent may be harder than 10×.

6.  Strategy drives ClarityDNA and sets the course for the future vision of the organization. It answers the questions, "Where we will play?" and "How

we will win?" The answers must be directional not theoretical, specific not general, and actionable.

7.  The pace of acceleration of business growth is directly correlated to the clarity of the strategic concept that drives it.

8.  Strategic clarity can be created at the top of the house, but cannot be implemented there. For a company to have high-growth performance, it must engage the entire workforce with clear expectations and assignments, spawning a new energy and enthusiasm for producing value.

9.  CommitmentDNA is the stage where value will be won or lost. How senior leaders behave, what and how often they communicate, and their ability to encourage two-way dialogue about the direction of the company will determine the success of the strategy.

10. CultureDNA may be the most challenging strand of all to address. It requires leaders to operate in a constant state of consciousness to avoid falling into hereditary habits. To sustain high performance over time requires a growth mindset to permeate the organization.

## KEY QUESTIONS

1. How confident are you in making bold decisions based on your market intelligence? Does it give you an "outside-in" look at the market?

2. How much clarity does your organization have based on its current strategy? Does it guide employees in what not to do as well as what is important?

3. How committed is your collective brain trust to achieving strategic goals? Do they know what they need to do to get the company there?

4. Does your organization have a growth-minded culture? Do all employees understand how to help deliver growth?

## CHAPTER 10

# GrowthDNA Is Cumulative

The four intertwined GrowthDNA strands are cumulative, each reinforcing the other. Much as in weaving, where fragile threads intertwine to produce strong cloth, GrowthDNA relies on all four strands to boost performance results. Woven fabrics are some of the strongest, due in large part to the over/under weave of the various threads. There is not just one thing that dictates the strength of the weave; factors that go into creating the strength of woven fabrics include yarn count, fiber density, and tightness of the weave.

In weaving, the lengthwise or longitudinal warp yarns are held stationary in tension on a frame or loom, while the transverse weft is drawn through and inserted over and under the warp. If there were not adequate tension on the loom, the weft could not be drawn tight and provide the necessary fabric strength.

With GrowthDNA, if there is not adequate data to generate leadership-wide Confidence-DNA in growth strategy, it is unlikely that there will be agreement, and the default is to focus on departmental operational improvements, thus suboptimizing performance against potential. If there is not sufficient ClarityDNA, defining

strategic direction, people won't understand what they are committing to, and will find it difficult to offer value-adding contributions even if they want to. Without substantial CommitmentDNA, great ideas will wane as support is spotty and new ideas surface. If CultureDNA isn't modified, it is likely that results will be moderated or less likely to be sustained. Boosting any one strand of GrowthDNA provides cumulative benefits across all DNA strands.

GrowthDNA is also cumulative over time. As leaders become more experienced in nurturing their DNA strands, they will find more and different ways to boost DNA—implementing new processes, behaviors, and ideas. These results are additive to the original benefits received in the first cycle of GrowthDNA. The higher the GrowthDNA, the better the company will perform. There is no ceiling for GrowthDNA, so the potential exists to take your company beyond where it is today, no matter how well it is already performing.

*While strengthening any one of the four GrowthDNA strands can have a positive impact on the business, all four are required for sustainable high-performance growth, year in and year out.*

It is valuable to understand the current levels of GrowthDNA in the organization. Without it, leaders run the risk of misdiagnosing what holds them back. The GrowthDNA Scorecard Assessment, a no-cost tool available at www.dnascorecard.com, is available to help you identify your organization's DNA code, and it gives you instant results (see appendix A for more information).

While strengthening any one of the four GrowthDNA strands can have a positive impact on the business, all four are required for sustainable high-performance growth, year in and year out. If there are three strong strands and one weak link, it is possible that all you may require is to focus on the underperforming strand to get a higher return out of all of them. If GrowthDNA reveals that all four strands have strengths and weaknesses, it might be best to start with boosting ConfidenceDNA and work around the cycle, strengthening as you go. The key is to know where you are now, and then you can determine how to strengthen your growth genetics.

## CHAPTER SUMMARY:

1. The four intertwined GrowthDNA strands are cumulative, each reinforcing the other.

2. While strengthening any one of the four Growth-DNA strands can have a positive impact on the business, all four are required for sustainable, high-performance growth, year in and year out.

3. If one strand is suboptimized, it can reduce the quality of results from the other three.

## KEY QUESTIONS:

1. How much time do you spend working on each of these four strands?

2. Who in your company is best suited to address and change the level of performance in each strand?

3. Are you interested in finding out your GrowthDNA score to identify where you are now?

## CHAPTER 11

# GrowthDNA Diagnoses Growth Limiters

Every organization has experienced business gravity. That gravity is what keeps your organization, and its performance, firmly rooted in place. Unfortunately, it can hold you down or limit growth. It is the gravity created by habits, the things that are routinely accepted as given—whether it is how we think, how we work, or how we behave. These habits are established over time and absorbed by new employees until they become the standard. They are usually self-created, but they are very difficult to change. Just like gravity—and DNA—they tend to be invisible, and are repeated without conscious thought.

> ∝
>
> *GrowthDNA can help organizations correctly diagnose growth gravity.*
>
> ∝

GrowthDNA can help organizations correctly diagnose growth gravity. Since companies pay attention to financial and operational results, they are usually quick to identify when performance is off. However, especially for low-GrowthDNA companies, the root cause of the problem is often misunderstood. Misdiagnosis is harmful, as it creates fruitless work, wastes valuable resources, and delays the right treatment.

Take a look at the GrowthDNA framework outlined below. The benefits from strong DNA in each strand is noted in the outside circle. If the organization is lacking in one of these outcomes, then the strand to be strengthened is the one that the benefit is associated with.

## GROWTHDNA FRAMEWORK

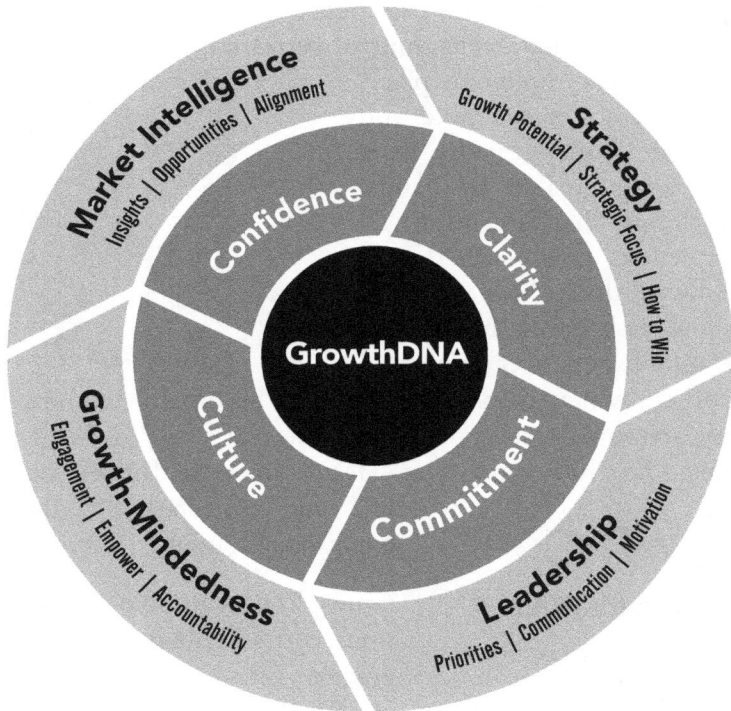

FIGURE 11.1

Following are some examples of business gravity that limit growth and the corresponding GrowthDNA strand that needs to be treated to resolve the issue.

**Does your company lack leadership alignment?** Do managers tend to thrive running their departments, but lack the interest or effort to lead their areas in support of the broader enterprise strategy? This isn't necessarily a commitment issue. They may be very loyal to the company and believe they are acting in its best interest. Rather, they lack confidence in the vision and are not aligned. The case for change hasn't been built, and they revert to where they have the most confidence—their own backyard. If the majority of your tracked metrics are operational or financial, you may lack sufficient market insights to develop confidence in a company vision. Build your ConfidenceDNA.

**Does your company have a strategic plan, but struggle with execution?** Chances are, leadership has not translated the plan into an actionable set of initiatives, has too many initiatives, has not funded them properly, or (most likely of all) has not communicated them adequately to motivate the troops. CommitmentDNA is lacking. Have you been disciplined enough to prioritize? While many things are important, major in the majors. Be sure you have answered the questions of how you will win as a company and where you will (and won't) compete. What will you say no to? Have you clearly communicated expectations? Are you communicating consistently and often enough?

> *While many things are important, major in the majors.*

**Is there always a battle over scarce resources with multiple departments competing for the same talent—most likely IT?** If so, there may be departmental objectives or goals rather than company-wide priorities. That is a result of lack of ClarityDNA. Develop company-wide priorities and ask departments how they will contribute. Limit the number of projects to those you can appropriately resource.

**Is there an issue sustaining momentum**? Culture may not be inclusive and growth-minded, with too few people involved in trying to transform the organization. Ask your employees what gets in the way of company success? How can leadership better support employees' growth and contributions? What type of ongoing communication is effective and helpful? Once you discover what is right, and not quite right, you can begin to implement new tools, practices, and processes which lead to new behaviors and strengthens CultureDNA.

Understanding the correct diagnosis for slow or blocked growth helps organizations boost the right DNA strand and realize improved results much more quickly.

## CHAPTER SUMMARY

1. Every organization has business gravity. It is the gravity created by habit or things that are routinely accepted as given—whether it is how we think, how we work, or how we behave.

2. GrowthDNA can help organizations correctly diagnose growth limiters. It isn't uncommon that when undesirable symptoms or behaviors are identified, the root cause of the problem is misunderstood.

3. The outcomes produced by each strand (as noted on the outer edge of the GrowthDNA circle) helps shed light on which strand might be holding you back.

## KEY QUESTIONS

1. Do you understand what unseen forces create your business gravity?

2. When is the last time you addressed a cause of business gravity?

3. Do any of the diagnosis examples given above surprise you? Did you think the problem was something different? Have you been mis-diagnosing a problem?

# PART 4

# The GrowthDNA Experience

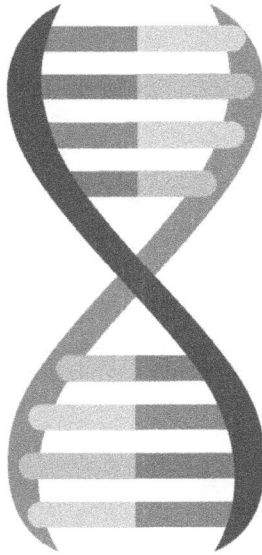

## CHAPTER 12

# GrowthDNA Case Studies

Those organizations with strong GrowthDNA look and act differently from other companies—and they get better results. High-GrowthDNA companies have become data-driven from an outside-in perspective, developed a focused and clear strategy, delineated and communicated priorities consistently to all stakeholders, and engaged the entire work force in achieving goals. Boosting GrowthDNA results in an organization confident in its bold long-term goals with clarity of direction, an aligned and committed leadership team, and a growth-minded culture that includes everyone in the organization.

GrowthDNA can be applied to any organization: businesses of all sizes, ownership types, and industries. While the types of challenges companies

>< 

*Boosting GrowthDNA results in an organization confident in its bold long-term goals with clarity of direction, an aligned and committed leadership team, and a growth-minded culture that includes everyone in the organization.*

><

experience may vary, the four strands necessary for success, along with the key behaviors and leadership practices linked to them, are similar.

Here are a few high-GrowthDNA client companies that have boosted their growth genetics to drive significantly improved and sustainable business performance.

## Confidence From Market Data: Travel And Transport

Travel and Transport, founded in 1946 as a private travel management company, has a long and successful history. While it does serve the consumer market, the company's focus is on domestic and international business travel for clients like T-Mobile, New York Life, and Kiewit Corporation. In 2002, the company became a 100-percent employee-owned organization and now has 1,800 people in forty-four states and four countries. In 2015, it was named the 2015 ESOP Company of the Year by the ESOP Association. In the last six years, it has tripled its share price. After that kind of success, it sounds like that could be the end of a great story; actually, it was just the beginning.

There is no question that the employee ownership of this company creates a strong culture which has been a market advantage of Travel and Transport's for some time. With employees having a stake in the company, they are encouraged to take personal interest in clients' satisfaction and to provide agile and responsive support to all customers. Travel and Transport takes pride in being a high-touch organization.

At the time we started working together, there was a confluence of two events: New leadership that desired greater strategic clarity, and disruptive market forces putting pressure on the existing model of the managed travel industry, which is growing at about 4 percent yearly. As with many industries, these shifts are accelerating and will impact the traditional avenues for growth.

Specifically, international travel is increasing at an expanding rate, and the infrastructure to accommodate it needs to keep up. Technology is an essential enabler in new product innovations that increase traveler convenience, as well as the efficiency of managing travel for both provider and client. As in every industry, client companies want more value for the dollar. While Travel and Transport is ranked in the Top 15 of *Travel Weekly's* Power List, at $3.2 billion in 2017 sales, they are far from the largest. Expedia holds that honor, with $88 billion in sales. Resources have to be deftly managed. Margin dilemmas are presenting themselves more often as market demands for this high-touch company to offer low costs escalate.

For Kevin O'Malley, who stepped into the CEO role in 2015, the fundamental question on the table was, can the company keep growing at this rate and if so, how? He needed the organization to determine what part of the company's historical model should be preserved, what should be challenged, what the best growth path to take was, and how it could be more deliberate in their growth and better manage where it applied limited resources. Before attempting to answer those questions, leadership conducted a deep dive into market and internal data.

Through market intelligence some important discoveries emerged.

**Customer focus and prioritization.** The data revealed that not all customers were created equally. Not all industries were experiencing the same growth regarding their travel needs, and it afforded Travel and Transport an opportunity to assess which industries with which they might establish more alignment. One consideration is understanding which industries have tailwinds. Growing customers will naturally increase their business volume, while those dealing with negative industry trends may shrink business travel.

**Service development and management.** As most services companies know, customers require the provider to develop interfaces for their systems that demand technological investments on behalf of the provider. Even more importantly, in this industry, they expect custom-designed services to track and manage their travel. Studying the correlation between amount of air travel, type of travel services needed, and/ or preferences for how travel services are delivered by the prioritized industry enables Travel and Transport to focus resources on the type of business travel services most valued by their prioritized segments, and thus align their high-demand technological capability where it can get the best return.

**Opportunities for differentiation.** If not all customers are created equal, then by default, they don't all have the same needs, and not all providers will win with the same approach. Travel and Transport knew going in that they were a high-touch company and technological innovation was an important key to the future. They had already developed apps, like Dash Mobile, and invested in DVI (Data Visualization Intelligence), which has the potential to lead the change in how travel business is managed. Thus, they had the opportunity to win by showcasing their strengths and saying no to prospects who were focused exclusively on the lowest price. For the first time, Travel and Transport didn't sweeten every deal with a red pencil but with innovation and valued services. Not every customer sees the value in that, but the right ones—the ones Travel and Transport could partner with most effectively for a long-term win-win—certainly do. In turn, that helps Travel and Transport better manage margin pressure. And those extra margin dollars can be reinvested in developing more innovative services for targeted customers.

**Market trends shape solutions.** There were at least three market trends that had a significant impact on how Travel and Transport chose to approach the market going forward:

- **Traveler-centric.** With more millennials in the work-force, there is a greater comfort with, and expectation for, the convenience of digital communication and real-time data management. Being available when the traveler needs something, focusing on the productivity of the customer on the road, and ensuring the traveler only travels when they really need to are important goals for a high-touch business supporting companies that value their employee's well-being.

- **Corporate productivity.** Who among us doesn't understand the value of increasing productivity through efficiencies? Travel is generally seen as an area of expense in companies, even though the purpose of travel is to generate a positive influence on revenue, often through more sales and better training. We all know that one of the first areas to get cut in an economic downturn is travel. Helping client companies improve their productivity is essential. Part of the transformation needed is to become more than a provider, but also a contributor to improved productivity through systems, technology, advice, and ideas. Getting travel partners to manage travel with an ROI mindset, which accounts for what is accomplished (not just what is spent), means conversations need to happen with leadership as well as accounting and logistics management—an opportunity to switch from the role of vendor to partner.

- **International.** With increased globalization, there is increased international travel. A number of technical considerations regarding the infrastructure are required to be an effective provider of international travel services. As mentioned above, not all industries have the same demand for international travel. In addition, business travel to some international markets is growing faster than to others. Travel and Transport is strategically increasing their capability of supporting high-growth global travel markets with a combination of acquisitions and partner development.

Travel and Transport used this analytical period to understand what data they had that they weren't using, as well as data they needed but didn't have. As a result, they are now making data-driven decisions.

What has changed?

**They now say no.** That may be one of the most difficult things a company can do. And it doesn't happen without an abundance of ConfidenceDNA. They have learned where their strengths lie and how to leverage them. They know that strategy is a choice, and they have made tough decisions and intend to stick with them. They are clear on which customers they can best serve; they understand where to invest scarce resources; and they understand the value of everyone in the organization working together on the same short list of high-priority projects. They have a new process to aid in prioritization and are learning to say no to the next shiny thing.

**They understand resource utilization.** They discovered where they were spending valuable resources with little return, and the potential impact of investing in fewer but more important products, markets, and systems.

**They have defined their competitive advantage.** Very few things make a company truly stand apart from its competitors. Most companies say the same things and provide the same services. Travel and Transport has done the hard work to determine how they are different, where they are truly unique, and how to build on that difference and create even greater separation between themselves and their competitors in their chosen market space.

What is the impact?

In 2018, Travel and Transport grew at more than twice the rate of other companies in their same space. To ensure effective implementation and results continue to meet or exceed goals, they have done some reorganizing, appointing a senior vice president and officer of strategy and communications. They are involving a much broader group of employees in the implementation stage, enlisting them on task forces responsible for strategic initiative development and implementation. Communication is an ongoing effort that will enable two-way communication about what is changing, why, and how employees can contribute.

> *"For many years, our company was very successful despite the fact that many decisions we made were more from the gut than based in fact or data driven. As we became larger, and our industry became more complex, we figured out we had to slow down a bit in order to speed up and make the right decisions. By taking the time to look at the data and then make strategic decisions, our ConfidenceDNA grew, and it really started making what had been hard decisions much easier."*
>
> **—Kevin O'Malley, CEO, Travel and Transport**

### Long-Term Strategic Clarity In A Shifting Environment: John Knox Village

John Knox Village is a life-plan-community founded in 1970. This not-for-profit organization is recognized as one of the most comprehensive communities of its type in the country. It provides independent living, countless services and amenities, and a full continuum of long-term health care services on its 400+ acre campus. The organization's vision is to be the leader among senior living communities in its market area.

A pillar in the industry and the community they serve, Lee's Summit, Missouri, John Knox Village led the way in responding to senior care trends and needs until the real estate crisis in 2009–2010. Like others in the heavily asset-based industry, leaders hunkered down for a few years as they overcame the many challenges faced across the board in their industry. By 2012, it was time to address some hard facts.

The lack of investment dollars available in the industry over the previous few years had left many behind the curve on addressing a rapidly changing target market with different needs. Seniors had become more active, with higher expectations for their living environments. If they weren't going to age at home, they wanted spaces that felt like home—larger, and with more amenities.

As a leader in the industry, it was important to John Knox Village to honor its vision and reinvest in being the leader in senior living. The extensive data analysis conducted on the front end— tracking industry trends, analyzing current property conditions and housing inventory, benchmarking other facilities—led to a courageous commitment to a long-term redevelopment plan that would not only bring the campus up to speed but also position the village to *wow* residents of the future.

The scope of the plan was significant. Not only were the leaders making up for lost time and had to move quickly; they also had a large campus to upgrade and needed to make highly visible moves that could change perceptions of the entire operation, while recognizing that the degree of change needed to respond to shifting trends in senior care expectations was significant. There was a sense of urgency, as competitors were building new sites that had the potential to dent John Knox Village's longstanding leadership.

The 2020 Plan was created to develop a comprehensive strategy for dealing with these challenges. The strategic work took a long, hard look at the existing business model before acknowledging that there was a more-than-adequate demand and revenue pool to continue to support the life-plan-community approach. Leaders spent countless hours redefining and tightening their target market and developing the financial model that was would be a win-win for them and their residents. They stopped managing each function of the community—independent living, assisted living, skilled nursing care, dining, upkeep, activities— as distinct functions and started looking at them as integrated services through the eyes of the residents who would live there. All of these areas had to work together to deliver the desired benefits. Changing one required changing others. Finally, it was also realized that *how* services were delivered mattered just as much or more than the facilities themselves. The plan included a commitment to a resident-centric hospitality culture.

Over the next year, leaders focused on taking ClarityDNA to the next level. They put together the work teams necessary to institute their plan for boosting their long-term performance and securing their leadership position. They developed a long-term campus redevelopment plan that phased the work over more than a decade. It includes multiple styles of housing, from villas to high-amenity condos. In the near term, they focused on high-visibility space that would signal the intent for the entire campus. And amenities were upgraded along with the living spaces to offer a commensurate lifestyle—more and better dining choices, a new theatre, and improved outdoor spaces. The new construction has been well-received and they are on track for implementation of the remaining facility development plan.

To ensure ClarityDNA was diffused throughout the entire organization and employees were knowledgeable about the future, leaders created an employee group, nicknamed P.R.I.D.E. (Personal Responsibility In Delivering Excellence), to drive their culture efforts. This rejuvenated culture has been integrated into hiring processes, behavioral training, and recognition programs. While always providing top quality services and healthcare, John Knox Village has raised the bar to meet the highest standards in their industry, preparing to secure status as one of the quality elite. The marketing message and pricing options were recrafted to appeal to their redefined target. The goal was to shift to an emphasis on long-term residents willing to invest in their future, known as entry-fee residents, rather than leasing residents.

Every year this organization further refines its strategy and takes the next step forward. This organization not only has had an extremely clear and detailed plan, phased out for over a decade, it has diligently worked the plan and is seeing results line up with goals in all facets of the organization.

Here are four areas of key results.

**Target resident mix.** John Knox Village has been successful in selling the preferred type of entry-fee contracts and has shifted the mix of entry-fee residents to 60 percent of move-ins in 2018, up from 20 percent in 2013—tripling the percent of new residents with long-term financial stakes in the organization.

**Operating margins.** With the new financial model, operating margins are forecasted at four times the level prior to redevelopment.

**Cash flow.** The organization has sequenced the plan to phase investments, managing cash and debt. New projects are undertaken as current projects reach financial targets.

**Resident and employee satisfaction.** Regularly conducted surveys show that satisfaction is up all around the campus, with employees and residents both referring more prospective residents to John Knox Village.

What is the impact?

When John Knox Village undertook a ten-year plan, they knew that the payout would not be immediate. There were some initial investment years while construction projects got underway. Buildings had to be torn down and new ones needed to be built before they could begin to reap the rewards. Throughout the planning period, John Knox Village has made progress in its leading indicator metrics, showing the plan is working. Six years in, it is on track to realize significant gains in margins and cash flows. Dan Rexroth, President and CEO of John Knox Village, reminds us that plan clarity encourages perseverance to see the plan through. Having a crystal-clear vision, along with well-documented success metrics and financial timelines, helps provide the courage to stay the course.

In the next few years, John Knox Village will continue to work the plan, completing current projects and undertaking new ones. The organization's leaders are cognizant that the senior living market is evolving quickly and are staying on the front end of changes. They challenge themselves to identify and evaluate the next round of *wow* ideas, whether those are additional amenities like a dog park or a hydroponic garden, technology applications, new trends in living like cohousing, or evolving health care with an emphasis on lifestyle living no matter what stage of health care is being provided.

*"I like things made simple. I like ideas described in black-and-white. Visionary talk is necessary when defining your purpose, but the rubber must eventually meet the road if you are going anywhere. I might modify Lewis Carroll's famous quote, 'If you don't know where you are going, any road will get you there' to, 'If you don't have strategic clarity, you will find your organization traveling down a lot of rabbit holes.' The greater the vision, the more clarity needed. People love a grand vision, but change and progress only happen*

> *through defining the strategy at a granular level so that everyone in the organization can understand it. One of my primary roles is to continue to help people internalize what our strategy is, our commitment to it, and how they can contribute. If you continually revisit or change your plan, you frustrate folks. Peace of mind comes from helping them understand that they are working on things that matter."*
>
> **—Dan Rexroth, President and CEO, John Knox Village**

## Leadership-Driven Commitment To Strategic Implementation: DEMDACO

DEMDACO has endeavored to put smiles on consumers' faces for over twenty years. The company works with artists to create a wide range of gift and décor items that lift the spirit of those who buy, give, and receive the products. A couple of its artist-inspired product lines include Willow Tree figurines designed by Susan Lordi, and Kitchen Boas, created by Laura Laiben.

For the first decade, most of DEMDACO's products were distributed through independent gift store retailers, but times have changed. The internet has become a much larger presence for both pre-shopping information as well as for purchases. In a recent study by Periscope by McKinsey, in all markets surveyed, at least 70 percent of respondents are undertaking some form of online shopping activity.[18] The exact impact varies by category, country, and age. "The survey shows that capturing the growing online consumer demand will require CPGs (Consumer Packaged Goods companies) to build out their digital capabilities for strong omnichannel strategies.

---

[18] "Periscope By McKinsey Announces Online Purchases in CPG Are Trending Up, Consumer Survey Shows," Periscope, by McKinsey, April 11, 2018. https://www.periscope-solutions.com/about-us/newsroom/full-press-release/periscope-by-mckinsey-announces-online-purchases-in-cpg-are-trending-up-consumer-survey-shows/.

CPGs should focus on managing both digital stores and key account relations for digital, including assessing online channel performance, understanding how consumers shop a category online, and identifying innovation opportunities from online trends. It requires the same rigor that has been applied to physical stores for years," said Brian Elliott, managing partner at Periscope by McKinsey.

Compound that with the challenge that comes from the advent of Groupon and other experiential gift-giving options, and companies that sell things in retail stores have had to rethink their growth strategies. Most are pursuing omnichannel strategies— meaning they must have multiple ways to reach consumers, which includes augmenting retail with an online presence.

Marketing to consumers is nothing like selling to retailers, as DEMDACO immediately understood. Branding, including product communication and messaging, must be developed to appeal to an end user as well as to retailers. Operationally, different packaging and shipping processes are needed. Perhaps most of all, this shift requires having a clear target: who the consumer is, how she lives, and what she wants. To become even more effective in today's market, DEMDACO began to rethink some of its traditional business operations and approach. Its leaders strengthened their commitment to defining and understanding their target end user.

In the last few years, they have spent considerable time not just defining her, but getting to know her. They have studied her and learned from her. They involve her in their product development efforts. And they seek to understand the emotional experiences she wants to give and receive—not just the product she wants to buy. They gathered information at an emotional and experiential level, understanding what makes her tick and motivates her to act. This process has inspired how they approach product development. For example, one of their new collections is named "Comfort, Uplift and Delight," and features art that celebrates friends, family, and nature from Sharon Nowlan.

Because of leadership's decision to become an omnichannel brand, they developed a short but significant list of seven key initiatives that would guide their strategic implementation. These initiatives involve what they make, how they sell it, and operational changes required. More importantly, they have an overarching and unwavering commitment to their new strategic focus—satisfying the end consumer—be that through retail distribution or online relationship development. If ever they find themselves stuck on a decision, they revert to asking, "What would she want?"

While the decision to focus on the needs of end users is strategically significant, DEMDACO did not change important aspects about the company and its culture. They still sell primarily through retailers and are committed to their success. Their unequivocal devotion to the end consumer only makes their product better and ensures sell-through, enamoring them to retailers who otherwise often end up owning unsold merchandise. Their longstanding culture of doing the right thing and being good community citizens is an outgrowth of the founder's belief that business is first and foremost a human endeavor.

The clarity of knowing what the brand stands for and who the end user is provided a laser focus that, in return, has boosted their CommitmentDNA. Steve Fowler, Chief Operating Officer and the leader for strategic implementation, said, "We have never had such commitment to a plan before. Everyone is energized, focused, and working hard to generate measurable results. Although we have high goals, we believe that we will achieve the objectives we set for ourselves."

So, what does that kind of extraordinary commitment look like?

**Aligned investment plan.** DEMDACO developed a funding plan that recognized the need to invest in new skill sets, new behaviors, and new processes.

**Project management visibility.** The company has a project management system in place to provide visibility to all high-priority initiatives and track progress against them as a leadership group. Leaders are accountable to each other for these enterprise-level initiatives.

**Established leading indicators.** Leaders developed a set of measures that were finely tuned to be leading indicators of strategic success, and they review them regularly. Different from the typical operational and financial metrics, which they still use, these metrics guide them strategically to ensure that their operational and financial progress directly link to the strategy of the organization.

**Communication planning.** Leaders have an ongoing communication plan that provides regular updates to employees on strategic progress, as well as solicits feedback for additional ideas and improvements that can be made throughout the organization. As a result, CommitmentDNA runs deep throughout the organization, as every employee knows their role in contributing to success.

What is the impact?

Although the traditional, small specialty store retail industry has been almost flat, growing at an annualized rate of 0.9 percent over the five years to 2018, DEMDACO is already seeing moderate growth in a segment of their business that has not been experiencing growth.[19] As it continues to get ahead

[19] "Small Specialty Retail Stores Industry in the US," IBISWorld, November 2018, https://www.ibisworld.com/industry-trends/market-research-reports/retail-trade/miscellaneous-store-retailers/small-specialty-retail-stores.html.

of product development cycle times and increase its consumer knowledge and its application to new product development, the company expects to see that trend continue and get stronger.

At present, the organization estimates it is about halfway through the implementation of the current plan. In addition to continuing to develop the key initiatives, it is working on ways to improve communication flow even more, particularly at the grassroots level, stimulating even more individual value-adding contributions.

*"This is not our first strategic plan effort, but the results are different. One of the biggest differences is the organization's commitment to the plan. This process enabled that in several important ways: (1) We included a broader group of influencers. (2) A communication plan was developed that includes diligently reviewing the strategic plan at town halls, in smaller groups, and cascading the message throughout our organization. (3) We review the key goals, initiatives, and related projects on a monthly basis with the responsible parties to ensure progress is in line with expectations. Those steps have contributed to the organization's awareness, engagement, and commitment to the plan, which are critical to long-term success and sustainability of the plan."*

**—Lance Hart, President, DEMDACO**

## Establishing A Growth-Minded Culture: Gray Manufacturing

Gray Manufacturing Company, Inc. has been designing, manufacturing, and selling lifting equipment for the automotive, truck, and service vehicle industries since 1952. This family-owned organization has deployed a fierce commitment to serving the customer with an eye for product innovation, driving a 25-percent increase in revenue in the last four years. Most companies would run with that all the way to the bank. But Gray wanted to answer a bigger question: What is our potential?

With the strengths they already had in place, company leaders were certain they could get to a whole new level of success. They were energized by the concept of growing twofold over the next planning horizon. They wanted to challenge themselves to be the best—in their industry, to their customers, and as an organization.

After eight months of data-diving and strategy formation, this organization is embracing the excitement and the initiatives necessary to drive that kind of growth. We just recently finished our last group meeting and recapped some important concepts that will guide the organization going forward, along with some of the key cultural shifts President Stet Schanze has already experienced because of their commitment to boosting GrowthDNA.

**Increased awareness and knowledge.** The data discussions that occurred when working on their ConfidenceDNA, have increased the awareness of key leaders across all functions regarding what drives the business, where money is made, and where opportunities lie. The group realized that serving customers is not just the responsibility of the sales division, but the goal of every team member. To do that, they need to be equipped with more knowledge regarding different types of customers and their needs, along with the organization's goals for each segment.

**Greater participation.** Along with more knowledge comes greater participation. There is a noticeable change with more people actively participating in important conversations. Because they are better informed with data, and clearer about priorities, they can then ask questions and contribute ideas, making discussions more meaningful and generating more unified confidence in decisions.

**Enterprise-wide initiatives.** From a strategic perspective, the organization shifted from developing functional or department-level initiatives designed to maximize existing operations to enterprise-wide projects, which elevate each department's contributions and advance the future of the business. As a result, there is more alignment among departments. Shared data puts more people on a level playing field, developing a unified understanding of what is important. Combine that with the establishment of common goals (enterprise-wide initiatives which focus on improving the company not just a specific department) and leaders and team members are now working together more often, at a higher level, and in a more collaborative way.

**More open-mindedness.** The number of initiatives identified are fewer in number but have much more potential impact. The organization's focus is creating an opportunity for resources to be aligned, for priorities to be clear, and for majoring in the majors. They are asking, "What can we stop doing that is tied to the past but doesn't advance the business, so that we can start investing in the things that will drive our future?" They are also asking, "What aspects of our successful past will continue to drive our future success?"

Schanze has also noticed that people are more open-minded and more willing to consider new ideas. Up until now, Gray has been very self-sufficient with great results. It rarely outsources, employing people in one plant location, scaling capacity as it goes. But new opportunities have surfaced after looking at the data; leaders have the potential to grow the company at extraordinary growth rates. Achieving this will require people to look at the business in an entirely different light, no longer stretching what is done to accommodate growth, but instead asking what will be necessary to enable the growth potential. Schanze likens it to the difference between looking at a golf hole from the tee versus looking back to the tee from the green. They are committed to reverse-engineering; now that they have defined their potential, they can ask what it will take to get there. That simplifies some things. Not all practices and processes come along for the ride. New ones are created. Some longstanding philosophies are changing. It is not easy, but people are open to those discussions, and that is where change starts.

It is still early in the process. This group hasn't even worked its way around the entire cycle. They have yet to directly address the culture and how they want to formally change processes, communication, accountability, and the like. Just by working through the first three strands, they have already realized significant cultural enhancements and have internalized that it is not what they do, but rather how they do it—their GrowthDNA—that will drive their future growth.

What is the impact?

They have confidently forecast an aggressive growth multiple for the next five years, which will take the organization to a completely different level of revenue while also strengthening their industry leadership in customer service, making them a formidable competitor and a sought-after employer. The ink on the plan isn't yet dry and they are already implementing it due to the clarity of direction provided by the strategy. They have already said no to smaller projects that they might have said yes to in the past, but now realize are distractions from accomplishing bigger goals. The organization is using a common language in the management ranks and is working more collaboratively than ever, planning on extending that alignment to front-line employees. It has implemented a more data-driven approach to decisions and also increased its delegation of decision-making.

The experience of their long tenured leaders is not replacing data, but is being enhanced by it. The dynamics have changed, enthusiasm is high, and prospects for growth are excellent.

> *"The GrowthDNA framework has pushed us to think differently while retaining and leveraging historical strengths and key company values. We were challenged to get out of our 10-percent-annual-growth paradigm and look at the possibilities of 2× or even 5× growth... and what it would take to get there. We have absolutely seen the value of getting out of departmental silos and getting into a one-enterprise mentality, with everybody working together to achieve enterprise goals. This makes it fun; we are all on the same team competing together rather than against each other. And it takes much of the unnecessary conflict and negative emotion, which undermines our ability to focus and holds us back from achieving our full potential as an organization, out of the process."*
>
> **—Stet Schanze, President, Gray Manufacturing**

Each of the above companies has made great strides in all four of the GrowthDNA strands. Each can see the difference in the organization and has developed behaviors, practices, and processes necessary to realize a higher trajectory of growth than it had before. Each is in a different stage of its journey. Regardless of whether it is still in the first cycle or has worked through several cycles, if it stays committed to boosting GrowthDNA, it will continue to see gains—in its *ConfidenceDNA* for bolder market moves, in the *ClarityDNA* of its strategic direction, in the *CommitmentDNA* of the organization to living the plan, and finally, to a more engaging, growth-minded *CultureDNA*. And the kicker? *Cultivating GrowthDNA is not a big financial investment like installing a new ERP or hiring more salespeople. It is simply a change in how organizations work every day.*

## CHAPTER SUMMARY

1. Regardless of the type or size of organization, it is possible to improve performance, drive growth gains, and sustain results using the GrowthDNA framework. This approach provides guidance to rethink how to lead the organization and achieve its true potential.

2. Maximizing success requires all four GrowthDNA strands working together, although improvements can be observed from the work in each strand.

3. Organizations can have strong cultures with great values, but might not be growth-minded without deploying some of the GrowthDNA principles.

## KEY QUESTIONS

1. Using the GrowthDNA framework, reflect on a company that you admire. Identify what strands are strong for them. What can you learn from that?

2. GrowthDNA requires leaders to accept that some practices and processes need to change to get better results. Change can require embracing some hard truths about past beliefs. Are you prepared for that?

3. After reading about the GrowthDNA framework, what do you think are the top four ideas you would like to implement in your organization?

# The GrowthDNA Scorecard Assessment

To boost your company's DNA the best place to start is understanding what its current GrowthDNA scores are. To determine what your organization's current DNA levels are in each of the four strands, take the free DNA Scorecard Assessment. It will give you a score for each strand in your organization so that you can discover where your strengths lie and which strands may be creating your limitations. It is available at www.dnascorecard.com, takes just a few minutes, and provides immediate results.

## Chart A.1: GrowthDNA Scorecard Assessment Questions

### ConfidenceDNA

| | |
|---|---|
| 1 | Does your organization make data driven decisions? |
| 2 | Do you have a robust data capture and reporting system that factors a variety of market and customer information into decision-making? |
| 3 | Does your company regularly share data across the organization to help align knowledge and decision-making? |
| 4 | Given the quality of the data available in your organization, do you have high confidence in decision making? |
| 5 | Does your data allow you to make bigger decisions without feeling they are more risky? |
| 6 | Do you have a detailed understanding of your customers' profitability? |
| 7 | Does your data tell you why your customers choose to buy from you over the competitors? |
| 8 | Do you measure success at all levels of the company by meeting or exceeding metrics? |
| 9 | Do you collect customer satisfaction information regularly? |
| 10 | Do your most valuable metrics include more than financials and operations? |

### ClarityDNA

| | |
|---|---|
| 1 | Can everyone in the organization easily define the strategy? |
| 2 | When asked to describe your strategy, does everyone in the organization use the same key words or phrases? |
| 3 | Are your organization's specific capabilities a true source of advantage? |
| 4 | Does your strategy put you ahead of trends? |
| 5 | Is your strategy specific about where and how to compete? |
| 6 | Does your strategy rest on proprietary insights? |
| 7 | Is your strategy free from historical bias? |
| 8 | Does your organization have a precise definition of high-priority target customers? |
| 9 | Does your strategy anticipate how technological advances will change the market and is flexible enough to accommodate for that? |
| 10 | Is your strategy long-term in nature? |

### CommitmentDNA

| | |
|---|---|
| 1 | Are the action steps required to successfully implement the strategy well defined? |
| 2 | Do you have a robust data capture and reporting system that factors a variety of market and customer information into decision making? |
| 3 | Does everyone in the organization understand how to contribute to strategic success? |
| 4 | Does the strategy forecast profitable growth at a rate exceeding the industry growth average? |
| 5 | Do you have and use metrics that provide an early indication of strategic success? |
| 6 | Are your interim metrics effective leading indicators of year-end financial performance? |
| 7 | Is the strategic direction clearly communicated to all in the organization regularly? |
| 8 | Has a communication plan for ongoing strategic communication been developed? |
| 9 | Is there a commitment to strategic implementation throughout the organization, at all levels? |
| 10 | Is there an effective tool or method for updating employees on strategic implementation progress? |

### CultureDNA

| | |
|---|---|
| 1 | Has the strategy been clearly communicated to all employees? |
| 2 | Does the process of strategic execution enable and encourage participation at the individual level? |
| 3 | Does the strategy influence how employees do their work every day? |
| 4 | Do employees understand the key criteria used in making strategic decisions? |
| 5 | Is decision-making dispersed throughout the organization rather than concentrated at the leadership level? |
| 6 | Does the organization regularly celebrate wins? |
| 7 | Are employees rewarded on results more than activities? |
| 8 | Does your company deploy "outside-in" thinking—or market-driven thinking—at all levels? |
| 9 | Is there sufficient bench strength for leadership positions? |
| 10 | Does strategy guide daily operational decisions? |

You will receive a report after you take the assessment that provides your scores along with some diagnostic information and suggestions to consider. You might also be interested in how your results stack up with those who have already taken it.

## Overall GrowthDNA Scoring

Just as every company has unique GrowthDNA, they have unique scores. There is a total possible of 200 points in the assessment. The highest score achieved so far has been 184. It was accomplished by a client I have worked with for almost a decade. The impact of applying these principles shows up not only in the assessment scores, but more importantly, in growth numbers. The average overall score for all assessment takers is 131. Most have not participated in GrowthDNA and are just starting on their journey. Approximately one-third are scoring 150 or better, and another 40 percent are in the danger zone, under 125. Most organizations will find GrowthDNA to be of great benefit to them.

## GrowthDNA Strand Scores

When the assessment is completed, in addition to the overall score, there will be a score for each strand, with a maximum of 50 points per strand. To make it simple to understand, each strand score is assigned a color: Green for 45 or more points, Yellow for 32–44 points, and Red for 31 or fewer points.

If you are scoring Green, you are performing that strand at a level that should be contributing to growth generation. If all four strands are Green, you are in a great position. Since the process is cyclical, you have the opportunity to continue to build on your strengths to pull further ahead of your competitors and accelerate growth further.

If the score is Yellow, your organization is doing some things very well and some things less well; the latter may be offsetting the advantages of the former. A deeper understanding of where the organization can improve is warranted.

If your organization scores Red, it is time to strengthen that strand, as it is most likely limiting potential growth. Any Red strand will undermine other strands, even if they are Yellow or Green.

What is fascinating about these scores is that the average for each strand is 33. What that tells us is that the average is pretty meaningless. The highest scores are in the upper forties; some scores are in the low teens. So, 33 is the average score because it is, well, the average. So, let's break this down.

**The strand with highest scores has been ClarityDNA,** with over one-quarter of respondents generating scores over 40. However, this strand also had the lowest scores, with 21 percent scoring under 25.

**CommitmentDNA is almost as polarized**, with 23 percent above a 40 and 18 percent below 25.

**CultureDNA is not the top-ranking strand**, with 21 percent of scores above 40, but it had fewer low scores with only 13 percent below 25. Scorecard takers have reported that what stood out to them in many cases is that they have a strong culture when defined by value systems and happy employees, but after taking the assessment, they realize that they have not connected the culture to business outcomes, which is generating the Yellow scores (some strengths and some weaknesses).

**ConfidenceDNA has the fewest high scores**, at 18 percent over 40, but also the fewest low scores, with 15 percent under 25. What makes this interesting is that while most scorecards reveal this to be average, this one strand has the most significant impact on the others. It is often the most misunderstood and misdiagnosed strand. It is likely pulling down scores and results of other strands.

## GrowthDNA Scores Correlate With Performance

When we compare scores of those who have completed at least one cycle of GrowthDNA from those who have not, we discover that those who have worked on their GrowthDNA have higher scores.

Score averages are eight to twelve points higher per strand for those completing GrowthDNA work over those who have not. The highest gap was in CommitmentDNA and the lowest in ClarityDNA. Since it is CommitmentDNA that drives strategic execution, and strategic execution creates value, it is not surprising that GrowthDNA correlates with boosted company performance.

Total scores for GrowthDNA participants are 26 percent higher than those who have not done DNA work.

## GrowthDNA Alignment Within A Company

One of the most interesting exercises is to have multiple people in the same company take the GrowthDNA assessment. It may show a range of opinions, or great alignment—both of which are helpful information.

In one company with four scorecard results, the totals ranged within four points of each other out of 200 possible—clearly a very consistent outcome. That company can rest assured they have alignment on where to put their efforts.

Another organization had a larger number of assessments completed across multiple levels in the company. Would it surprise you to know that the lower in the company, the lower the scores? How about learning there was a 100-point swing in scores? This is an organization that may be doing things right in some strands, but the entire organization isn't privy to that information, indicating that CommitmentDNA and CultureDNA need to be addressed.

GrowthDNA is what separates those organizations able to achieve sustainable results year after year from the rest. To be clear, the DNA isn't the function or skill, like market intelligence or strategy. Rather it is the C connected to it—ConfidenceDNA, ClarityDNA, CommitmentDNA, and CultureDNA. These Cs are the organic characteristics that are embedded in an organization. They are not skills that are taught in business school. They are there as a result of how leaders lead.

Every organization has the opportunity to strengthen their GrowthDNA by changing how the organization thinks, decides, and acts. It requires a conscious approach that starts at the top of the company and weaves its way through every action, every decision, and every communication.

What will your GrowthDNA Scorecard Assessment show about your organization? Take the GrowthDNA assessment here: www.dnascorecard.com

# Chapter Summaries

## Chapter 1

1. While growth is an important goal for most companies, only a small minority of them (approximately 13 percent) are effective at sustaining growth over time.

2. The rise in intrinsic equity value from a 1-percent increase in growth is about five times larger than the same increase in pretax operating profit.

3. Even growth-oriented leaders spend the majority of their time focused on operational improvements and financial management and much *less* time on growth initiatives.

4. As leaders, it is critical we spend as much or more time studying and understanding the market trends and behaviors than examining our internal functions.

## Chapter 2

1. Strategic planning often doesn't yield growth.

2. Strategic planning, like other management tools, is often viewed as a process, not an outcome.

3. Growth is the result of the way an organization undertakes activities, not the activities themselves.

4. Every organization has DNA that influences *how* they get things done; it is the DNA that separates those which are successful from those which are not.

## Chapter 3

1. Knowing your DNA, personal or organizational, helps you understand how you are wired, which in turn enables you to proactively manage and even change the outcomes.

2. GrowthDNA is a framework designed to help leaders identify the variables in their organizations—the DNA—that contribute to or detract from the growth of the company.

3. GrowthDNA testing reveals that awareness of organizational DNA can lead to substantially improved DNA results.

4. There is an alignment between GrowthDNA scores and high-performance organizational growth.

5. GrowthDNA consists of four DNA strands:

   a. ConfidenceDNA: Confidence comes from using market data to challenge the status quo, deciding what to build on, where weaknesses are, and what new opportunities exist.

   b. ClarityDNA: Clarity comes from crafting a specific, well-defined strategy that is clear to all in the organization.

   c. CommitmentDNA: Company-wide commitment begins at the top and is the number one goal of leadership.

    d. CultureDNA: It is CultureDNA that enables organizations to sustain growth year after year.

## Chapter 4

1. Relentless market pressure often requires the organization to take a different approach—an outside-in approach—to developing growth strategy and solving daily business problems.

2. A fast-growing trend that is adding new revenue streams to traditional manufacturers is the addition of services.

3. Market intelligence helps you identify gaps in the market that align with organizational strengths and gives companies the confidence to think and act boldly, delivering on the first strand of GrowthDNA.

4. Market intelligence should include macro, industry-specific, and company-specific data.

5. Companies with strong market intelligence make bolder decisions as they are buoyed by having indisputable facts upon which to make decisions.

6. Factual data helps align perspectives across functional areas, minimizing emotional or experiential biases.

## Chapter 5

1. Strategy answers the question of how an organization will win in the market.

2. The right question with which to lead strategy development is "What is our potential?"

3. Clarity of strategy is as important as the strategy itself. In order for strategy to take root in an organization and

serve as a driver of performance, it must be understood by everyone involved in its implementation.

4. Clear strategy is like a funnel, with the broadest strategy decisions at the top. The following strategic decisions are included:

    a. Overarching strategy

    b. Strategic positioning

    c. Value proposition

    d. Target customer

    e. Product/Service offerings

5. Strategy is different from what a company makes; rather, it defines what impact the organization is trying to have on its customers.

6. Strategy needs to be unique to your organization, directional at an enterprise level, broad enough to encourage scalability, and specific enough to be clear.

## Chapter 6

1. GrowthDNA leaders need to be coaches and encourage employees to get in the game. Developing buy-in and encouraging contribution at an individual level is central to success.

2. When growth plans fail, it is usually due to poor execution. Those organizations that succeed still lose, on average, 37 percent of projected value associated with strategic plans.

3. Only one of every four strategic growth initiatives return value. The most common reasons are:

a.  Initiatives are not fully vetted.

b.  The impact on human capital resources is not considered.

c.  Priority projects don't receive adequate funding.

4.  To increase the odds of successful growth results:

   a.  Identify strategic initiatives on company level, not department level.

   b.  Limit the number of total high-priority initiatives in a given time frame.

   c.  Reward employees for results, not activities.

   d.  Allocate appropriate resources for project success.

   e.  Communicate priorities clearly, consistently, and visibly.

## Chapter 7

1.  CultureDNA is critical as it drives sustainability.

2.  Culture is the collection of behaviors of an organization—derived from shared attitudes, values, goals, and practices—that characterize an institution or organization.

3.  A strong culture can have a dramatic impact on the performance of an organization. The Gallup organization states that nearly 70 percent of employees are actively disengaged. According to Deloitte, 94 percent of executives believe that a distinctive culture is connected to success but fewer than one in three executives (28 percent) report that they understand their organization's culture. Forbes shares that companies with strong cultures saw a 400 percent increase in revenue growth.

4. GrowthDNA companies have a growth-minded culture. Characteristics of this culture include:

   a. **Alignment** across functional areas and effective teamwork at all levels of the organization.

   b. **Transparent** understanding of the key components of strategy and the growth plan across all levels of the organization, not just leadership.

   c. **Strategic specificity** that ensures all stakeholders understand how the strategy impacts their role.

   d. **Clear priorities** linked to resource allocation guide investment and day to day work.

   e. **Informed** employees that understand the current performance of the business.

   f. **Dispersed decision-making** means employees are training to solve problems and to do so they must understand the strategy, financial performance, marketing trends, and operational processes.

   g. **Inclusiveness** encourages employees to contribute ideas and solutions not just identify problems.

   h. **Active communication,** which includes two-way communication, is the norm.

5. The keys to a growth-minded culture are awareness of what is needed, communication that motivates action, and accountability for all to drive results.

## Chapter 8

1. The sequence of GrowthDNA matters, as it impacts the outcome, much like the order of letters create a word. Furthermore, DNA—human and business—can be genetically modified to achieve a different, better outcome.

2. Best outcomes occur when all four strands are strong and functioning interdependently.

3. The strands—ConfidenceDNA, ClarityDNA, CommitmentDNA, and CultureDNA—interconnect in three ways:

    a. They are cyclical: There is a logical starting point and the cycle never ends.

    b. They are cumulative: Each strand builds on the one before.

    c. They are diagnostic: They provide the ability to diagnose the root cause of issues that limit growth.

## Chapter 9

1. The initial engagement point for those wanting to build GrowthDNA is ConfidenceDNA. Without it, other actions around the circle are typically more incremental in nature, with less impact, and are often under-resourced.

2. Most leaders attempting to drive improved performance mistakenly start with CommitmentDNA. It is

in this phase that operational execution is challenged, scoped, and defined. They ask the question, "How can we be better?" instead of the more growth-oriented question, "What is our potential?"

3.  Outside-in means looking at the company just as those outside of it—customers, competitors, or market analysts/investors—would. It also means looking at the market with fresh eyes, unrestrained by internal operational legacy.

4.  As the organization works through the entire cycle, better understanding the value of the data and how to deploy the data in decision-making, more support builds for identification and development of data-capture and -analysis systems. And that is true of all the strands—GrowthDNA builds over time.

5.  It is a common self-limiting belief that 10× is not in the cards and the company should be thrilled with a 10 percent increase. In fact, the case can be made that 10 percent may be harder than 10×.

6.  Strategy drives ClarityDNA and sets the course for the future vision of the organization. It answers the questions, "Where we will play?" and "How we will win?" The answers must be directional not theoretical, specific not general, and actionable.

7.  The pace of acceleration of business growth is directly correlated to the clarity of the strategic concept that drives it.

8.  Strategic clarity can be created at the top of the house, but cannot be implemented there. For a company to have high-growth performance, it must engage the entire workforce with clear expectations and assignments,

spawning a new energy and enthusiasm for producing value.

9. CommitmentDNA is the stage where value will be won or lost. How senior leaders behave, what and how often they communicate, and their ability to encourage two-way dialogue about the direction of the company will determine the success of the strategy.

10. CultureDNA may be the most challenging strand of all to address. It requires leaders to operate in a constant state of consciousness to avoid falling into hereditary habits. To sustain high performance over time requires a growth mindset to permeate the organization.

## Chapter 10

1. The four intertwined GrowthDNA strands are cumulative, each reinforcing the other.

2. While strengthening any one of the four GrowthDNA strands can have a positive impact on the business, all four are required for sustainable, high-performance growth, year in and year out.

3. If one strand is suboptimized, it can reduce the quality of results from the other three.

## Chapter 11

1. Every organization has business gravity. It is the gravity created by habit or things that are routinely accepted as given—whether it is how we think, how we work, or how we behave.

2. GrowthDNA can help organizations correctly diagnose growth limiters. It isn't uncommon that when undesirable symptoms or behaviors are identified, the root cause of the problem is misunderstood.

3. The outcomes produced by each strand (as noted on the outer edge of the GrowthDNA circle) helps shed light on which strand might be holding you back.

## Chapter 12

1. Regardless of the type or size of organization, it is possible to improve performance, drive growth gains, and sustain results using the GrowthDNA framework. This approach provides guidance to rethink how to lead the organization and achieve its true potential.

2. Maximizing success requires all four GrowthDNA strands working together, although improvements can be observed from the work in each strand.

3. Organizations can have strong cultures with great values, but might not be growth-minded without deploying some of the GrowthDNA principles.

# Chapter Key Questions

## Chapter 1

1. What is your company's growth track record? Is it meeting or exceeding the average for your industry?

2. How much of your time (and that of other key people) is focused on managing day-to-day operations versus driving growth initiatives? Are you satisfied with that distribution of your most valuable asset—time?

3. To what extent does your organization routinely examine the "why" behind the "what"? In other words, do you approach growth by building on what you have, assuming that extending the past is the answer—or do you look at what the market is telling you and define what is possible for your organization before setting goals and objectives?

## Chapter 2

1. How effective has your organization's strategic planning been when measured by results?

2. Is your strategic planning work a static, occasional process, or does strategy drive day-to-day work?

3. Can you define your organization's DNA?

## Chapter 3

1.  Which of the GrowthDNA strands do you think would be your organization's strength?

2.  Which of the GrowthDNA strands do you think would be your organization's weakest link?

3.  How growth-minded do you think your culture is?

## Chapter 4

1.  Does your organization make data-driven decisions?

2.  Do you have a robust data capture and reporting system that factors a variety of market and customer information into decision-making?

3.  Does your company regularly share data across the organization to help align knowledge and decision-making?

4.  Given the quality of the data available in your organization, do you have high confidence in decision-making?

5.  Does your data allow you to make bigger decisions without feeling they are more risky?

6.  Do you have a detailed understanding of your customers' profitability?

7.  Does your data tell you why your customers choose to buy from you over the competitors?

8.  Do you measure success at all levels of the company by meeting or exceeding metrics?

9.  Do you collect customer satisfaction information regularly?

10. Do your most valuable metrics include more than financials and operations?

## Chapter 5

1. Can everyone in the organization easily define the strategy?

2. When asked to describe your strategy, does everyone in the organization use the same key words or phrases?

3. Are your organization's specific capabilities a true source of advantage?

4. Does your strategy put you ahead of trends?

5. Is your strategy specific about where and how to compete?

6. Does your strategy rest on proprietary insights?

7. Is your strategy free from historical bias?

8. Does your organization have a precise definition of high-priority target customers?

9. Does your strategy anticipate how technological advances will change the market and is flexible enough to accommodate for that?

10. Is your strategy long-term in nature?

## Chapter 6

1. Are the action steps required to successfully implement the strategy well defined?

2. Are resources allocated in a manner consistent with the strategic priorities?

3. Does everyone in the organization understand how to contribute to strategic success?

4. Does the strategy forecast profitable growth at a rate exceeding the industry growth average?

5. Do you have and use metrics that provide an early indication of strategic success?

6. Are your interim metrics effective leading indicators of year-end financial performance?

7. Is the strategic direction clearly communicated to all in the organization regularly?

8. Has a communication plan for ongoing strategic communication been developed?

9. Is there a commitment to strategic implementation throughout the organization at all levels?

10. Is there an effective tool or method for updating employees on strategic implementation progress?

## Chapter 7

1. Has the strategy been clearly communicated to all employees?

2. Does the process of strategic execution enable and encourage participation at the individual level?

3. Does the strategy influence how employees do their work every day?

4. Do employees understand the key criteria used in making strategic decisions?

5. Is decision-making dispersed throughout the organization rather than concentrated at the leadership level?

6. Does the organization regularly celebrate wins?

7. Are employees rewarded on results more than activities?

8. Does your company deploy "outside-in" thinking—or market-driven thinking—at all levels?

9. Is there sufficient bench strength for leadership positions?

10. Does strategy guide daily operational decisions?

## Chapter 8

1. Does your organization struggle to get the return it expects from its growth investments?

2. Does your organization feel like employees aren't as engaged as they need to be?

3. Which of the four strands do you think creates your biggest challenge?

## Chapter 9

1. How confident are you in making bold decisions based on your market intelligence? Does it give you an "outside-in" look at the market?

2. How much clarity does your organization have based on its current strategy? Does it guide employees in what not to do as well as what is important?

3. How committed is your collective brain trust to achieving strategic goals? Do they know what they need to do to get the company there?

4. Does your organization have a growth-minded culture? Do all employees understand how to help deliver growth?

## Chapter 10

1. How much time do you spend working on each of these four strands?

2. Who in your company is best-suited to address and change the level of performance in each strand?

3. Are you interested in finding out your GrowthDNA score to identify where you are now?

## Chapter 11

1. Do you understand what unseen forces create your business gravity?

2. When is the last time you addressed a cause of business gravity?

3. Do any of the diagnosis examples given above surprise you? Did you think the problem was something different?

## Chapter 12

1. Using the GrowthDNA framework, reflect on a company that you admire. Identify what strands are strong for them. What can you learn from that?

2. GrowthDNA requires leaders to accept that some practices and processes need to change to get better results. Change can require embracing some hard truths about past beliefs. Are you prepared for that?

3. After reading about the GrowthDNA framework, what do you think are the top four ideas you would like to implement in your organization?

# APPENDIX D

# Works Referenced

Lewis Carroll, *Alice's Adventures in Wonderland*. Church Hanborough, Oxford: Artists' Choice Editions, 2009.

"Culture of Purpose-Building business confidence; driving growth, 2014 core beliefs and culture survey." Deloitte. com, 2014. https://www2.deloitte.com/content/dam/Deloitte/us/Documents/aboutdeloitte/us-leadership-2014-core-beliefs-culture-survey-040414.pdf.

"DNA and Mutations." Understanding Evolution. University of California Museum of Paleontology. https://evolution. berkeley.edu/evolibrary/article/mutations_01.

"Genetic Screening and Support for Women and Their Families." Myriad Women's Health. https://evolution.berkeley. edu/evolibrary/article/mutations_01.

Jim Harter, "Employee Engagement on the Rise in the U.S." Gallup.com, November 21, 2018. https://news.gallup. com/poll/241649/employeeengagement-rise.aspx.

Kotter, John, "Does Corporate Culture Drive Financial Performance?" Forbes. Forbes Magazine, June 23, 2012. https:// www.forbes.com/sites/johnkotter/2011/02/10/doescorporate-culture-drive-financial-performance/#5898b-f507e9e.

Lewis, Michael. *Moneyball: the Art of Winning an Unfair Game*. New York: W.W. Norton, 2013.

Mankins, Michael. "Stop Focusing on Profitability and Go for Growth." Harvard Business Review, September 20, 2017. https://hbr.org/2017/05/stop-focusing-on-profitability-and-go-for-growth.

Michael C. Mankins and Richard Steele, "Turning Great Strategy into Great Performance," Harvard Business Review, July 2005. https://hbr.org/2005/07/turning-great-strategy-into-great-performance.

Marquet, L. David. *Turn the Ship Around! How to Create Leadership at Every Level.* Austin, TX: Greenleaf Book Group Press, 2012.

"New Survey Finds Majority of Americans Want to Know What's in Their DNA." Business Wire, September 24, 2015. https://www.businesswire.com/news/home/20150924005346/en/New-Survey-Finds-Majority-Americans-What's-DNA.

"Periscope By McKinsey Announces Online Purchases in CPG Are Trending Up, Consumer Survey Shows." Periscope by McKinsey, April 11, 2018. https://www.periscope-solutions.com/about-us/newsroom/full-press-release/periscope-by-mckinsey-announces-online-purchases-in-cpg-are-trending-up-consumer-survey-shows/.

Regalado, Antonio. "2017 Was the Year Consumer DNA Testing Blew Up." MIT Technology Review, February 13, 2018. https://www.technologyreview.com/s/610233/2017-was-the-year-consumer-dna-testing-blew-up/.

Reynolds, Margaret. "Services, Not Products, Drive Next Wave of Growth for Manufacturers." Breakthrough Masters, Unlimited https://www.breakthroughmaster.com/2019/03/services-not-products-drive-next-wave-of-growth-for-manufacturers/.

"Small Specialty Retail Stores Industry in the US." IBISWorld, November 2018. https://www.ibisworld.com/industry-trends/market-research-reports/retail-trade/miscellaneous-store-retailers/small-specialty-retail-stores.html.

"What Is DNA?" U.S. National Library of Medicine. National Institutes of Health. https://ghr.nlm.nih.gov/primer/basics/dna.

Zook, Chris. *Beyond the Core: Expand Your Market without Abandoning Your Roots*. Boston, MA: Harvard Business School Press, 2004.

# Acknowledgments

This book would not have happened without the support and encouragement of some very talented people. You have heard the expression "You are the composite of the people you spend time with"? Well, I try to hang out with smarter and brighter people who make me better. This book is one result.

After a meeting of the Cigar PEG Key West Mastermind Group, an educational and philanthropic group affiliated with the National Speakers Association, I returned to the office with my mind percolating, full of many good ideas and a challenging question: How could I better define what separates high-performance companies from the rest? To most of my colleagues, I am considered a strategic planning expert. And perhaps I am. But that is not how I view the world. Strategy is simply a means to an end. I view myself as a growth catalyst; someone who can help companies realize growth opportunities they didn't even know they had. It is important to me to continue to find new ways to champion more growth for client companies, and strategic planning contributes to that result.

But even good strategy doesn't separate high-performance companies from others. What distinguishes high-performance companies from the rest is not just one thing, one skill, or even a great culture. How could I build a framework based on my life's work that captured the essence of high-performance companies?

At about the same time I was struggling with this question, I decided to give DNA kits to my adult children for Christmas.

And the rest is history, as they say.

I became inspired by the idea of business DNA. It became glaringly obvious looking back over years of data that it is not activities that separate high-performance companies, it is their approach to how they execute those activities. It is strategic leadership that imbues four key characteristics (DNA) into their organizations over time. From that point of inspiration, we began collecting empirical evidence through the GrowthDNA Scorecard Assessment, which has affirmed the correlation between GrowthDNA and business performance.

So, my heartfelt thank you and appreciation to all of you who inspired me to create this framework and helped me document it in this book.

To my Cigar PEG buddies, Ed, David, Ray, Dawnna, Mary, Annalisa, Robert, Daniel, Peter and the rest, thank you for asking tough questions and sharing your brilliant insights.

To my clients and colleagues, too numerous to list individually, whose experiences taught me so much and whose long-standing friendship is my greatest reward.

To my publisher, Henry Devries, for insisting I write the book and not take short-cuts; for encouraging me throughout the process with his enthusiasm for the topic and content; and for helping me get it out the door quickly, since once I commit, I go fast and hard.

To all those out there with curious minds who ask the tough questions and inspire others like me to ask them, too.

To my assistant, Melissa Buchanan, who never thought she would help pull a book together, and probably didn't want to, but did an amazing job.

To my family, who support me every day and who stoically tolerate my passions, hobbies, and work habits.

To Roman, my first grandchild, and a window to a whole new world.

# APPENDIX F

# About the Author

Margaret Reynolds is the founder and owner of Breakthrough Masters Unlimited, a division of Reynolds Consulting, LLC. Reynolds is a recognized expert at helping middle-market companies identify and implement next-stage growth. Her work is industry-agnostic. She has clients of all ownership types, including public, private, family-owned, ESOPs, and nonprofits. Her great success in bringing strategic discipline and creativity to her widely varying client portfolio has demonstrated the universality of the growth principles she has developed over her career. Many of the stories shared in this book showcase her clients' tremendous success in applying them to their businesses.

Reynolds began her career at Hallmark Cards, Inc., where she held executive roles of general manager and lead strategic officer. She was known for her natural inquisitiveness and innovative inclinations, never resting with the status quo. Reynolds Consulting, LLC was founded in 2001, within days of the 9/11 event, which are indelibly etched on her mind.

An established author, Margaret published *Reignite: How Everyday Companies Spark Next Stage Growth* in 2015, available on her website and Amazon. Prior to that, she authored a three-book minibuk series titled *Master Breakthrough Growth Series,* which can be found on her website: https://www.breakthroughmaster.com/bookstore/. She has authored columns and articles for various magazines, including the *Kansas Business Journal,* the *Nashville Business Journal, Mergers and Acquisitions Magazine, Speaker* (the magazine of the National Speakers Association), and many others. Her weekly blog is distributed around the world.

She is a sought-after speaker known for her creative ideas and practical advice in the areas of leadership, strategy, marketing, and growth. Her expertise is tapped by organizations from Fortune 500s, such as Hallmark Cards, Inc. and Tractor Supply Company, to diverse mid-market companies such as Travel and Transport, DEMDACO, Cramer Products, John Knox Village, and Flood, Bumstead, McCready and McCarthy.

Reynolds delights in her hobby of competitive trail riding as a member of the National Association of Competitive Trail Riding (NATRC) and has won back-to-back National Championships on her horse VA Caradelle. The sport combines endurance riding with trail obstacles to challenge the rider and horse to achieve effective conditioning and maximum teamwork. Like running a business, competitive trail riding requires a plan, dedication, and preparation, along with disciplined orchestration of implementation.

That passion has led to numerous adventures riding horses across rural land in countries around the globe. Reynolds has ridden Andalusian horses in the Catalonia mountains of Spain, Boerperds in the African veldts of Botswana, Arabian stallions in the Sahara Desert of Morocco, Shagya Arabs across the fields and forests of Romania, and most recently, the great Marwaris through Rajasthan, India. A story of her most recent adventure can be found at OutdoorJournal.com.

# Index

*Alice in Wonderland*, 58

Amazon, 30, 33, 42, 44

Amazon GO, 33

Apple, 29-30, 39, 43

Ask, don't tell, 61, 84

Brown, Kevin, 53

Budget planning, 10

Business DNA, 18-19

Changing the leadership approach, 58

ClarityDNA, 20-21, 24, 39, 41, 44, 59, 69-72, 78, 85, 89, 96, 109, 120, 126-128, 130, 135-136

Collective brain trust, 22, 81-82, 87, 143

CommitmentDNA, 21-22, 24, 47, 50, 53, 69-73, 81-82, 85-86, 90, 95, 114-115, 120, 126-128, 130, 135, 137

Communication, 18, 21, 43-44, 51-53, 55, 61-63, 65, 96, 105, 107, 113, 115-116, 119, 128, 134-135, 142

Company economics, 35

Competitive advantage, 82, 106

Competitive strategy, 34

ConfidenceDNA, 20, 24, 27, 32-33, 35, 69-74, 77-78, 81, 85, 89, 91, 95, 106-107, 117, 120, 126, 128, 130, 135

Consumer Packaged Goods companies, 112-113

Corporate productivity, 105

CultureDNA, 22, 24, 57, 64, 69-72, 82-83, 86, 90, 96, 120, 126-128, 131, 133, 135, 137

Customer Focus and Prioritization, 103

Customer value shifts, 34

Dash Mobile, 104

Data Visualization Intelligence, 104

Decision-making, 32, 37, 58, 60, 65-66, 77-78, 85, 119, 134, 136, 140

DEMDACO, 112-116

Demographic and value trends, 34

Department level goals, 10

Develop company-wide priorities, 96

Economic Markets, 34

ESOP Association, 102

ESOP Company of the Year, 102

Ford, 44

Fowler, Steve, 114

Gravity (business, growth), 93, 95-97, 137, 144

Gray Manufacturing Company, Inc., 116

Groupon, 113

GrowthDNA scorecard assessment, 19, 22, 90, 123-124, 128

GrowthDNA Strands, 20, 23, 25, 89, 91, 120-121, 137-138, 140

Growth initiatives, 5, 7-9, 48, 50-52, 54, 62, 129, 132, 139

Growth-minded culture, 58, 62-65, 87, 101, 116, 134-135, 143

Hallmark Cards, Inc., viii, 44

How we win, 21, 23, 39-40, 45, 136

Industry concentration, 34

John Knox Village, 107-108, 110-112

Kiewit Corporation, 102

Kitchen Boas, 112

Lagging indicators, 5

Laiben, Laura, 112

Leadership alignment, 23, 95

Leading indicators, 5, 55, 115, 142

Lee Jeans, 44

Lee's Summit, Missouri, 108

Lexus, 42

Lordi, Susan, 112

Macro trends, 20, 33

Market Intelligence, 11, 20, 22, 27-28, 30, 32-33, 35-36, 41, 70-71, 74-75, 78-79, 81, 83, 87, 103, 128, 131, 143

Market Trends Shape Solutions, 104

McKinsey, 112-113

New York Life, 102

Nowlan, Sharon, 114

O'Malley, Kevin, 103, 107

Omaha Steel Casting Co., 53

Operational and growth metrics, 5

Opportunities for differentiation, 104

Outside-in, 20, 27, 35-36, 66, 75-77, 83, 85, 87, 101, 131, 136, 143

Patagonia, 40, 42

Plastic Enterprises, 75-76

Power of teamwork, 61

Rexroth, Dan, 111-112

Santa Fe Railroad, 44

Schanze, Stet, 117-120

Southwest, 39

Srinivasan, Ramji, 17

Steele, Richard, 48-49, 52

Strategy:

  funnel, 40, 45, 59, 132

  overarching, 10, 39-41, 45, 59, 132

Strategic:

  implementation, 10, 55, 112, 114, 142

  leadership, 150

  planning, 9, 11, 13, 78, 129, 139

  thinking, 18

  trends, 34

Target end user/target customer, 42-43, 45-46, 59-60, 113, 132, 141

Technological capabilities/technology, 33, 104

Ten percent vs. 10x, 79

T-Mobile, 102

The Gallup organization, 57, 64, 133

Travel and Transport, 102-107

Travel Weekly's Power List, 103

Traveler-centric, 105

Value proposition, 41, 43, 45, 132

Walmart, 40, 42

Where we play, 80, 85, 136

Willow Tree figurines, 112